DRIVEN BY PURPOSE

Your Practical Guide to Discovering
Individual and Team Purpose and
Mobilising it into Positive Impact

by

Mushtak Al-Atabi

*Author of "Think Like an Engineer" and
"Leading with Stories"*

DREAM BIG. BE DIFFERENT. HAVE FUN.

ISBN: 978-967-13063-3-8

Published by:
Mushtak Al-Atabi
Heriot-Watt University Malaysia
No 1, Jalan Venna P5/2, Precinct 5
62200 Putrajaya, Malaysia

Illustrated by:
Janice Chaw Zhi Ting

www.thinklikeanengineer.org

Praise for Driven By Purpose

"It was an enlightening experience to undergo the Impact Statement process with my team from the Nicol David Organisation, guided by Professor Mushtak Al-Atabi. This process provided me with a profound perspective, emphasising the importance of exploring values that resonate with me as a foundation for understanding my purpose more deeply. Having individuals who know me well participate in the process was invaluable, as their insights contributed to helping me craft an Impact Statement that feels truly personal and meaningful to embrace in my life. I truly appreciate Professor Al-Atabi for facilitating this experience with my team."

Nicol David
Founder and Head Coach, Nicol David Organisation
Ex-World Champion for Women Squash

"I had the privilege of participating in Mushtak's Impact Statement Workshop which involved empowering exercises and skilful coaching that provides one with the tools to crystallise and articulate one's purpose. It was truly enlightening to discover my own purpose at the workshop on a day which also happened to be my birthday! I am delighted to see that Mushtak has translated this transformative experience, that many have gone through, into a book, ensuring that more people can access and benefit from this life-altering work. Regardless of where you are in your life or career, I fully recommend that you make the commitment to discovering your purpose, this may end up being your most impactful undertaking."

Gopalan Rajagopalan
Head of Tata Consultancy Services, Scotland

"As a strategy scholar, I am familiar with the idea that underlying purpose is important for organisations and leadership teams. Professor Al-Atabi's groundbreaking work on Impact Statements takes this idea and applies it to each of us individually. Working with Mushtak to develop an Impact Statement helped me to focus on what mattered to me, my motivation for the work I do and how I use those insights to frame interactions with others. I'd highly recommend it as an exercise."

Professor Robert MacIntosh
Pro Vice-Chancellor, Northumbria University

"I found the process of articulating my Impact Statement to be grounding and thought-provoking. It invites you to be curious about your life's purpose in a deeply personal but practical, valuable and enlightening way. It crystallised many thoughts and experiences into something impactful and galvanising."

Sian May
Head of School, Alice Smith School

About
The Book

This is a book about your purpose and how to find, articulate, and develop the commitment to pursue it. It is intended to be a workbook that contains exercises designed to help you discover your superpowers, express your purpose, and affirm your actions to mobilise your purpose into a positive impact on the world. The first part of the book concentrates on the development of individual purpose and impact, while the last chapter describes how the same philosophy and methodology can be used by teams, businesses and organisations to convey their institutional purpose and plan the delivery of their collective impact.

Contemplating the awe-inspiring journey of human progress across the last ten millennia—from mastering fire and creating the wheel to unlocking the power of the atom and pioneering Artificial Intelligence—I am firmly persuaded that our next and ultimate challenge lies deep within us. Discovering and mobilising our purpose is the ultimate frontier in leadership, parenting, and human flourishing in general. This conviction holds particularly true in an era where advanced technology disrupts our world, emphasising the urgency of asserting the unique value that humans contribute to life.

The methodology and exercises described in this book have evolved over the past decade as they have been successfully utilised by thousands of people of all ages and stages and many teams and organisations to articulate their purpose and develop plans to mobilise it into a positive impact on the world.

I assume that you got this book either because you want a straight-to-the-point way of finding your individual or team purpose or because someone who believes in you and/or in your team gave it to you. With this in mind, the book is written with as little text and theory as possible and designed to provide ample space for reflection and learning. However, the introductory sections provided are meant to satisfy the needs of readers who might be interested in the theory and the foundational stories behind some of the concepts and exercises described here. By the end of the process, when you fill in the spaces provided, answer the questions, and complete the reflections, the book will be truly personalised for you. A short chapter on crafting a purpose-driven life is provided to outline a methodology that you can use to ensure alignment between your articulated Impact Statement and the life endeavours that you are pursuing. You will be able to refer to the book repeatedly as your purpose journey evolves and your impact story matures.

About
The Author

Professor Mushtak Al-Atabi is currently the Provost and CEO at Heriot-Watt University Malaysia. A passionate educator, innovator and an agent of change, Mushtak always challenges the status quo to unlock value. He pioneered the use of the CDIO (Conceive, Design, Implement, Operate) educational framework in Malaysia. He offered one of the first Massive Open Online Courses (MOOCs) in Asia (the first in Malaysia) in 2013. His online classes, *Entrepreneurship, Success with Emotional Intelligence and Global Entrepreneurship,* attracted thousands of students from 150 countries. He speaks at international conferences and consults for national and multinational corporations, including universities, banks and manufacturing and energy companies, in the areas of leadership, innovation, human development, performance and technology. Mushtak is the author of *Think Like an Engineer and Driving Performance.* His research interests include thermo-fluids, renewable energy, biomechanical engineering, engineering education and academic leadership. He has numerous research publications, awards and honours. Mushtak is a Fellow of the Institution of Mechanical Engineers (UK), a member of the Board of Directors at the British Malaysia Chamber of Commerce and the Chairman of the Vice-Chancellors' Council of Private Universities in Malaysia.

Mushtak
Al-Atabi

" I am a storyteller. My purpose is to inspire people to tell more empowering stories about themselves and the world we live in. "

My Impact Statement

Mushtak Al-Atabi

CONTENTS

Introduction

As part of my work as an educator, professor, and provost, I regularly speak to rooms filled with parents and young students exploring their post high school university options. I often start my talks by asking this question: "Who is not sure what to do with their future and what course of study to choose?" Usually, 95% of the students' hands go up, often to the dismay of their parents.

This state of not being sure what to do with one's life is not unique to the young. Speaking to business leaders, they often refer to the lack of motivation, commitment, and loyalty among their employees as being linked to a scarcity of connection to the sense of meaning and purpose, both individual and organisational. In 2017, we developed a programme for all students and staff at Heriot-Watt University Malaysia to participate in; so that they could develop their "Impact Statements." These are statements that articulate their superpowers, purpose, and the actions they intend to undertake to mobilise their purpose into a positive impact on the world.

This work has been very well received by students, their parents and even employers and community leaders who, on multiple occasions, asked us to facilitate Impact Statement workshops for their leadership teams and their boards of directors. As we continued this work, we started receiving requests from teams and organisations to help them articulate their organisational Impact Statements. We adapted the Impact Statement development methodology creating a version that could be used by a group rather than individuals and the results were truly remarkable. The team Impact Statement methodology is also described in this book. It is highly recommended that the team Impact Statement is developed only after all the team members develop their individual Impact Statements.

Victor Hugo said, "There is only one thing stronger than all the armies of the world: and that is an idea whose time has come." At a time when the intellectual superiority of humans is challenged by Artificial Intelligence, the sources of stress and anxiety are plentiful, and the challenges we face are global and existential, knowing one's purpose stands as the bedrock for sustainable human existence, ensuring human success, and aspiring towards human flourishing. I strongly believe that the importance of discovering and articulating purpose and impact is an idea whose time has come.

With technological advancements such as Artificial Intelligence and machine learning leading to increasing proportions of physical and cognitive work being automated and fulfilled by machines, the disruption to the economy, job market, education, and society will be deep and far-reaching. This will make personal purpose discovery an even more important requirement for success and flourishing in life. I predict that in the not-too-far future, students will go to schools and universities primarily to learn about themselves, discover their purpose, and build plans to mobilise it into a positive impact on the world, and secondarily to learn about a disciplinary body of knowledge such as engineering, accounting, or medicine.

This book is designed to take you through the same process and exercises that thousands of people of all ages and at all stages in life and careers have been through to discover their purpose and gift it to the world.

How to Use
This Book ?

When developing an Impact Statement under the guidance of a trained Impact Coach, the process can take anywhere from 3 to 5 hours of intense work. This can be done continuously or over 1 to 3 sessions. If you are working on this book at your own pace, you have the flexibility to choose how to progress based on your circumstances. However, it is highly recommended to tackle this work continually with minimal long breaks or interruptions.

Ideally, each component – the "I am" Statement, Purpose Statement, and Actions Statement – is completed in a focused and uninterrupted manner, allowing for periods of reflection and collaboration with others in between.

Impact Statement workshops are usually done in groups of 5-10 participants guided by an Impact Coach. When doing the work using this book, it might be good to explore if another individual would like to embark on their purpose journey simultaneously with you. Having a partner can make the journey even more fulfilling and enjoyable.

While you can embark on this work at any age or stage in life, pursuing purpose remains a lifelong endeavour. Hence, you may revisit the exercises in this book in the future to reflect on your purpose and impact journey. This can have a nice record of your evolution and progress. While doing this, keep in mind that this is a workbook, so feel free to fill it with your own work, writings, and reflections and even add more pages if the space is not sufficient.

After completing your Impact Statement, you may sense a need for further alignment between your purpose and the life endeavours you are undertaking, that is why the chapter on crafting a purpose-driven life will come in handy. It outlines a straightforward methodology that can help you achieve that.

If you are interested in helping your team or organisation develop their collective Impact Statement, the last chapter is for you. Remember that it is highly recommended that team members complete their personal Impact Statements first before embarking on developing their team or organisational statements.

1

Why Purpose?

"The two most important days in your life are the day you are born and the day you find out why."

-Mark Twain

We have always known the importance of having a clear sense of purpose and awareness of what brings meaning to our lives. Philosophical, spiritual, and human development practices focused on the importance of purpose for the good life.

Friedrich Nietzsche believed that the primary objective of philosophy is to guide us in becoming our true selves, driven by a profound yearning to discover the purpose of our lives. Viktor Frankl, the Austrian neurologist, psychiatrist and Holocaust survivor, demonstrated that having a sense of purpose can even help in surviving the concentration camps. During World War II, Frankl and his family were captured by the Nazis and sent to various concentration camps, including Auschwitz. Despite enduring unimaginable suffering and witnessing the horrors of the Holocaust, Frankl managed to survive by finding a profound sense of purpose and meaning.

While imprisoned in the camps, Frankl observed that those prisoners who held on to a sense of meaning and purpose were more likely to survive. He realised that the will to find meaning in one's life, even in the most dire circumstances, was a powerful force. Frankl noted that those who gave up hope and a sense of purpose were more likely to succumb to the brutal conditions and despair of the camps.

Frankl's own survival was a testament to his own philosophy. He held onto the belief that his life had a purpose, even within the walls of a concentration camp. He mentally and emotionally disconnected himself from the immediate suffering and focused on a future beyond the camp, where he could share the insights he gained from his experiences.

After the war, Viktor Frankl wrote about his experiences in his famous book "Man's Search for Meaning."[1] In this book, he described his time in the concentration camps and his philosophy of logotherapy (logos means "meaning" or "reason" in Greek), which emphasises the importance of finding meaning in all forms of existence, even in the face of suffering.

Viktor Frankl's story is a powerful illustration of the human capacity to find meaning and purpose, even in the most horrific circumstances. His work continues to inspire and influence psychologists, therapists, and individuals around the world, reminding us of the resilience of the human spirit and the importance of having a sense of purpose in life.

More recently, the work of William Damon[2], a Stanford professor, established the importance of having a sense of purpose for youth for success, well-being, and overall positive development. However, Professor Damon's work pointed towards a deficit of purpose as his research pointed out that "only about one in five young people in the 12-22 year age range express a clear vision of where they want to go, what they want to accomplish in life, and why."

Robert Quinn, the organisational scholar and co-author of "The Economics of Higher Purpose,"[3] outlined the importance of purpose for organisations and how becoming a purpose-driven organisation is the pathway to business success, career satisfaction for employees, and deeper engagement with customers.

A 2020 McKinsey Survey[4] exposed an interesting "purpose gap" between executives and upper management staff, where 85% agree they can live their purpose in the day-to-day work, compared to 85% of frontline managers and employees who either were unsure or disagreed that they can live their purpose at work. This represents an important area for leaders to work on and improve as bridging this gap can translate into a direct improvement in productivity, creativity, and goodwill.

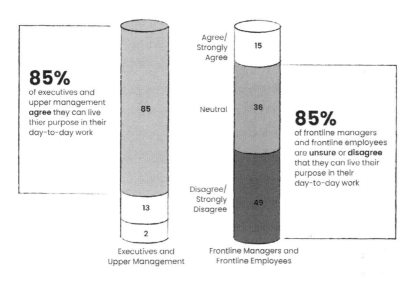

The Purpose Gap

There is now a compelling body of research indicating that those with a clear sense of purpose, defined as a stable and generalised intention to accomplish something that is at once meaningful to the self and consequential to the world beyond the self, are healthier, happier, and more successful.

A Brief History of Human Civilisation

Humans experience life, shape their environment, and interact with each other via three essential capacities or labours; our physical labour, cognitive labour, and emotional labour. We use these three labours to process materials, energy, and information to create systems and objects and deliver services with the intention of adding and creating value.

In this section, we will tell the story of our civilisation, from the invention of the wheel to the development of AI, as seen through the lens of the three human labours. This has been a journey that culminated in the age of purpose that is dawning upon us and it is depicted in the figure below and explained thereafter.

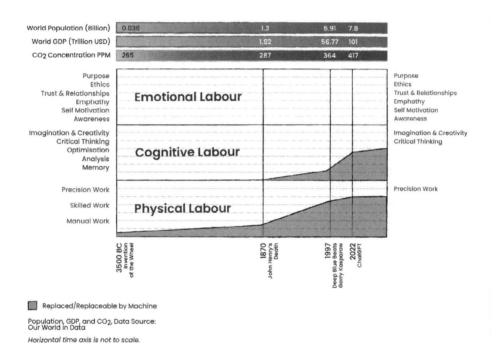

History of our Humanity, Work, Technology, and Impact

Whether we are cooking a meal, writing a book, making a sandcastle, building a piece of furniture, constructing a house, or manufacturing a car, we are essentially using some form of energy to reshape and put together materials, concepts and ideas according to desired and imaginative patterns. The patterns in which materials and/or ideas are put together can generally be referred to as the information content of the system we are constructing. Generally speaking, the eventual value of what we produce depends on the cost and value of the materials, energy, and information needed to produce it. The rarer and the more difficult to acquire the required materials and the more original, restricted, and complex the information content of a system, the more valuable it is. Information needed to make or produce something refers here to the knowledge, experience, skills, and imagination that go into making it. If the produced item is a unique piece of art, then the value of the artist's distinct style will be scoped here too introducing subjectivity into the evaluation. Energy is usually more fungible, so the more energy we use to produce something the more costly it gets.

We use these three labours simultaneously in different proportions depending on the mission or task we are undertaking. This is how we apply ourselves in the world and collectively impact it while impacting ourselves in return. Remember, this classification of the labours does not imply that they occur independently of each other. For example, we need our cognitive capacities and our nervous system to control our muscular system to perform even the most mundane of physical tasks. We also need our emotional capacities to keep ourselves motivated to perform physical and cognitive tasks.

Each of these three labours exists on a growing scale of complexity. The physical labour, which refers to our ability to move and manipulate objects and depends largely on our muscular strength and dexterity, can manifest itself as routine manual work such as sweeping the floor or carrying some loads, skilled work as in bricklaying, or precision work as in tuning a piano. The cognitive labour is founded on the bedrock of the cognitive capacity, memory, which is demonstrated by the ability to memorise and recall knowledge and information. The cognitive labour complexity progresses to include analysis of information, optimisation, decision-making, critical thinking, and ultimately creativity and imagination which are the pinnacle of human cognitive achievement. The emotional labour deploys skills and capabilities such as awareness, self-motivation, empathy, relationship-building, a sense of purpose and meaning, and behaving ethically.

Since the dawn of time, humans worked on enhancing how these labours are delivered and deployed. This usually starts with improving humans' personal capability to deliver the labour, by working towards becoming stronger, faster, and generally more effective. If the work is dangerous, dull, or difficult, or when human biological limits to process materials, energy, and information are reached, people start to look for alternatives to extend themselves, so the labour is either mechanised if the technology is available or transferred to domesticated animals to perform it. This trend is particularly obvious with the physical and cognitive labours. Humans started by enhancing physical labour, they always wanted to be able to carry and move around increasingly heavier objects and do that at a higher speed; think of the stones used to build the pyramids of Giza. To achieve that, humans invented the wheel, used levers and ropes, and employed draft animals. They also harnessed nature's energy using inanimate objects such as sails, water wheels, and windmills. All of that raised the capacity to use energy to process materials to a whole new level. From the time the wheel was invented in Mesopotamia circa 3500 BCE, the gradual inclination towards replacing human physical labour with mechanical labour intensified. Machines free humans from the limitations that biology imposes. A human body, or the body of a draft animal like a horse, elephant, or ox for that matter, unlocks the energy contained in food through the metabolism process and uses muscles to deliver physical labour. A steam engine or an internal combustion engine, on the other hand, can process and release massive amounts of energy and use that to deploy huge sums of physical labour, fueling the building of civilisation at an unprecedented scale. The First Industrial Revolution in the 19th century culminated in the accelerated deployment of machines that were far stronger and much faster than any human being or domesticated animal. This was accompanied by a major loss of manual human jobs and a great deal of disruption to the social and political order.

A watershed moment that represented the essence of the disruptive nature of the First Industrial Revolution is the story of John Henry. John Henry was an African American strong man who lived in the middle of the 19th Century. He worked as a steel driving man, hammering steel chisels into rocks making deep holes to place explosives to dig tunnels for the Chesapeake and Ohio railroad. He was the best at his job, driving one steel chisel after another as they were blunted and replaced by his partner. During his working days, steam-powered hammers started to appear, these were brought to compete against John Henry, and he always won. The power of steam seemed to be no match for the strength and dexterity of the human muscle. One day in 1870, the engineers working on the railroad brought in the latest steam-powered digger to compete against John Henry. A man-against-machine race started. At the end of the race, John was able to dig 14 feet, while the machine managed only 9 feet. However, this would be the last time any human could beat a machine at such a mainly physical task, as John Henry collapsed and fell dead at the end of the competition.

Throughout the First Industrial Revolution, machines continued to improve in effectiveness, efficiency, and reliability and human jobs that were based on physical labour kept on being mechanised. Not only were many jobs lost, but the disruption had also far-reaching consequences on the very fabric of nature and society, transforming our reality politically, economically, socially, and environmentally. In the industrialising nations, many people migrated from rural areas to urban industrial centres to get jobs in the newly built factories. The notion of wealth, which was locked in the value of land for millennia since the Agricultural Revolution, transformed to increasingly include the ownership of the means of mass production, creating a new capitalist class. The richest people were no longer the feudal owners of large swathes of land but rather the capitalists who owned factories, railroads and concessions for the coal mines, and later, oil fields that fueled the Industrial Revolution. This served as the background for rapid growth in the volume of economic exchange, human population, environmental pollution, and inequality.

Educational institutions expanded their offerings to cater for the needs of the industry, and massive exercises of upskilling and reskilling of the workforce took place. The educational outcomes focused on enhancing and expanding human capability to deliver cognitive labour, as increasing amounts of physical labour were being carried out by machines.

While the trends of increasing mechanisation, urbanisation, economic growth, human population, inequality, and environmental degradation continued throughout the 19th and 20th Centuries, the scientific and technological developments of calculating and computing machines were happening simultaneously. Starting with mechanical calculators that were able to perform simple calculations, computers kept improving in performance and speed while reducing in size and price and increasingly being able to perform tasks within the cognitive labour domain. For a start, computers have a superior memory compared to humans, a trend that is only increasing by the day. They are able to retain, process and analyse massive amounts of data, and with the right computer programmes, they are even capable of learning and discerning trends much faster than us. Once again, machines are enabling humans to transcend their biological limitations. Despite all of this, many experts thought that cognitive labour would remain largely the human territory where we create and add superior value.

Just like in the case of John Henry, our superiority was due to be unforgivingly tested. In May of 1997, human cognitive supremacy was put to the ultimate trial when Gary Kasparov, the world champion in chess, played a chess rematch against Deep Blue, an IBM supercomputer in New York City. The 6-game rematch came after a similar set that was played between the human master and the supercomputer in Philadelphia in 1996 when Kasparov won 4-2. However, the programmers of Deep Blue were able to make changes and improvements to the code and the rematch was won by Deep Blue 3½ – 2½. A tight win, but it created another watershed moment, nonetheless.

Computers have come a long way since 1997, and the field of Artificial Intelligence and the ability to harness and process Big Data held the potential to dominate wide aspects of the cognitive labour domain and transform the jobs market. A 2017 study by McKinsey and Company[5] predicted that by as early as 2030, 800 million people could lose their jobs while 375 million people will need to undergo a career change as a result of technological advancements.

With the release of ChatGPT in November of 2022, which is the latest conversational Artificial Intelligence (AI) large language model developed by OpenAI, the tale of displacing humans in the cognitive domain enters a whole new chapter. You can ask ChatGPT to write you a speech, a computer code, a report, a song, an essay or even a whole book in a matter of seconds. The capabilities of this technology will only grow wider, deeper, and stronger, challenging us to justify the value we can add in the area of work.

The enormous acceleration in the ability to store, process, and learn from data and information changed the nature of the economy again. Today the largest, richest, and most influential companies are not the behemoths of manufacturing with their large number of employees and huge physical assets but rather information technology, often cloud-based, companies such as Apple, Microsoft, and Google. The consolidation of capacities in these cloud-based companies is transforming them into platform monopolies with powers similar to those of landowners in the feudal system. Yanis Varoufakis, the economist and ex-finance minister of Greece, considers this stage a post-capitalism one and calls it technofeudalism[6].

These staggering advancements coincided with substantial economic progress, witnessing global gross domestic product (GDP) surge from USD 1.92 trillion in 1870 to approximately USD 101 trillion in 2022. The human population also experienced significant growth, expanding from 1.3 billion in 1870 to surpass 7.8 billion in 2022. However, this progress was accompanied by escalating environmental pollution, exemplified by the rise in atmospheric CO_2 concentration from 287 PPM (parts per million) in 1870 to 417 PPM in 2022.

According to the Science Information for Climate-Smart Nation website (climate.gov), the current level of atmospheric CO_2 is the highest the earth has experienced in the past 800,000 years. The last time the atmosphere contained such high levels of CO_2 was 3 million years ago, during the Mid-Pliocene Warm Period. Back then the temperature was 2-3°C higher than the temperatures of the pre-industrial era and the sea level was 15-20 meters higher than today.

The Age of Purpose

Clearly, the contemporary world is simultaneously defined by unparalleled challenges and rapid technological progress. Artificial Intelligence (AI) is poised to expand significantly in terms of its power, scope, and impact. At this nascent stage, financial institutions are already leveraging AI to evaluate risks and determine who gets a loan and who doesn't. AI stands apart from conventional technologies; it represents the first instance where a piece of technology can autonomously learn and enhance itself beyond human oversight. This characteristic marks a paradigm shift, as all prior human technologies, regardless of their sophistication, have remained subject to human control. Nuclear bombs, for example, are unable to build more nuclear bombs and they cannot choose to deploy themselves without a human decision. Nick Bostrom, the Swedish-born Professor of Philosophy at Oxford University who founded the Future of Humanity Institute, has long predicted that, in the not-too-far future, computers will be more intelligent than humans, achieving what he calls "superintelligence"[7].

The big question is, as computers develop superintelligence, how can we be sure that this won't end in disaster, as already being predicted by some of the world's smartest minds? How will computers know how to behave? This might sound like a science fiction question, but it is one that deserves consideration, alongside the regular questions about jobs to be lost to automation and other economic and political questions surrounding Artificial Intelligence.

Professor Bostrom's view, elaborated on in his TED talks, books and papers, is that we need to be confident that when superintelligent AI escapes the control of humans, it remains safe. He says that we need to ensure that AI "is fundamentally on our side because it shares our values." But how do we make machines share our values? This will require a paradigm shift towards an area that we, rather than the machines, are superior at, our emotional labour represented by our sense of purpose, value system, self-awareness, and emotional intelligence.

After all, machines learn from Big Data sets that are generated by us. They include the content we create and the behavioural breadcrumbs that we leave behind as we surf the net and make choices and decisions. When training Amazon's Alexa using content available on the web, a team of researchers from Heriot-Watt University discovered that Alexa developed a nasty personality. It is now very well established that AI algorithms (e.g.

the ones used to select the right people to hire) pick up human biases in decision-making, even when humans are unaware of these biases themselves.

Even Garry Kasparov who lost to Deep Blue in 1997 now advocates the development of protocols and skills that enable humans to work collaboratively with intelligent machines. "We must face our fears if we want to get the most out of technology—and we must conquer those fears if we want to get the best out of humanity," says Kasparov.

In an era where machines are poised to assume significant roles in both physical and cognitive tasks, environmental degradation reaches unsustainable historic levels, and in the face of geopolitical and health challenges, along with rampant inequality, it becomes imperative to contemplate how we can sustain our relevance, motivation, productivity, and our ability to collaborate across national and group boundaries. We must also work together to ensure that our technologies remain safe and dedicated to helping us address the grand challenges of our age. These are the profound questions that will define our contemporary existence and answering them will require developing shared purpose and mutual trust.

A lack of shared purpose and mutual trust between competing nations will almost certainly result in weaponising AI. This will have dire consequences that we cannot afford. At the risk of sounding naïve or idealistic, I do not see any solution to this dilemma other than investing in the development of a deep sense of true purpose at the individual, organisational, societal, and national levels.

During the First Industrial Revolution, humans were able to control machines thousands of times stronger than themselves, because they were cognitively superior. To prepare for a world in which machines are cognitively stronger than us, we need to ensure that we are able to fully develop our ultimate domain, our emotional labour. This will require the commitment to discovering and articulating our purpose and the dedication to aligning our personal, professional, and organisational objectives with this purpose to ensure that we can mobilise it into a positive impact on the world.

A key advantage of having a clear sense of purpose is that it cultivates a hopeful attitude and a long-term perspective. This can provide the antidote for the dichotomy between the short-term thinking prevailing in business and politics where performance is measured in quarters and election cycles, and the long-term thinking required to address the complex grand challenges we face today, such as climate change, where improvements demand commitment on a very long timescale.

Just like how the Agricultural Revolution and the subsequent Industrial Revolutions were catalysts for us to take our existence and understanding of ourselves to a whole new level, we need a Human Revolution to reach our ultimate frontier through investing in developing ourselves, our communities, and our organisations to be purpose-driven. This way, we can create a world that is sustainable, equitable, and enjoyable. I trust that the purpose and impact journey that you will embark on through this book will help you be ready to be an active contributor in this age of purpose.

2

Your Impact Statement

"True happiness is not attained through self-gratification, but through fidelity to a worthy purpose."

-Helen Keller

Knowing who we are, discovering our purpose, and having plans to mobilise this purpose into a positive impact on the world can be life-transforming.

A powerful and inspirational way to express a sense of purpose is by articulating an Impact Statement. This statement has three parts: the "I am Statement," the "Purpose Statement," and the "Actions Statement." At my university, we made it a requirement for all new students to reflect on how they want to make the world a better place through their work, talents and the programme of study they choose. Coming up with an Impact Statement is never easy, and it takes a lot of one-to-one interactions with our Impact Coaches. However, we found that the effort and time invested in writing an Impact Statement at the beginning of a student's first semester pays multiple dividends. Students who are aware of why they started studying a certain subject are more likely to stay the course when the going gets tough.

When we ask students why they join our Actuarial Science programme, for example, they often say that they love mathematics and that having a degree in actuarial science will secure them a good job. After completing the Impact Statement exercise, students are clearer about their true north. One of them wrote, "I am a math lover. My purpose is to use my mastery of math to reduce complexity for others when they need it the most. I am an actuary." How is that for an Impact Statement?

When we cast a stone in a lake, a ripple effect is generated. This can be big or small, short or long-lasting depending on the size of the stone, the strength with which it is cast, and also how it was thrown. In the figure below you can see 3 concentric circles. Imagine these circles as the ripple effect that your existence causes in life. When we know who we are, we can build a strong first wave on which we build our purpose wave, this in turn can be the basis of highly impactful actions on the world.

Self-Awareness, Purpose, and Impact

In this chapter, the structure of the Impact Statement is briefly described. As mentioned earlier, the Impact Statement has three parts, I am Statement, Purpose Statement, and Actions Statement. This is shown using the word IMPACT as an acronym below.

Impact Statement Structure

In the following chapters, we will go through step-by-step exercises to articulate the three parts of your Impact Statement as shown in the roadmap below. While the process may look sequential, it will also be iterative and non-linear. The process we will use has been tested by thousands of individuals of all ages and backgrounds to find their Impact Statements, so all I ask of you is to follow the instructions, trust the process, and enjoy the journey.

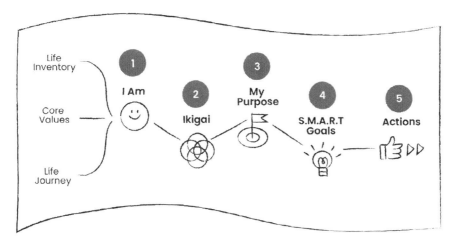

Roadmap for Writing Your Impact Statement

3

Finding your Superpower

"Becoming a leader is synonymous with becoming yourself. It is precisely that simple, and it is also that difficult."

-Warren Bennis

Self-knowledge is the ultimate knowledge. That is why, the Impact Statement starts with an "I am" Statement that describes the essence of who we truly are. Knowing who we are and being able to clearly articulate that, will empower us to become who we are and provide a strong foundation for our behaviour and sense of purpose. At its core, leadership is the process of discovering and becoming who we truly are so that we can gift our superpowers to the world.

To reflect on who we are, we will do 3 exercises; taking stock of the inventory of our life, discovering our core values, and reflecting on our life journey.

Life Inventory (M.E.R.S.V.P.)

In this section, you will examine and rate yourself on 6 important dimensions: mentally, emotionally, relationally, spiritually, and vocationally (M.E.R.S.V.P.). These dimensions are briefly described below:

▶ Mentally: The state of your mind and intellect—Are you learning and growing intellectually?

▶ Emotionally: Your affective state of consciousness—How aware are you of your emotions and are you handling emotions appropriately?

▶ Relationally: The quality and state of your relationships—Are your relationships healthy and happy?

▶ Spiritually: Do you feel connected to a bigger cause or meaning?

▶ Vocationally: Your job, career, or studies—Do you feel satisfied, are you growing in these areas?

▶ Physically: Your body and health—Are you healthy and fit? Do you consume a healthy diet? Do you have sufficient exercise and sleep?

Let's work:

1. On the diagram below, rate yourself on each one of the dimensions from 1 (poor) to 10 (excellent).

2. Connect the points on each dimension to create your flourishing map.

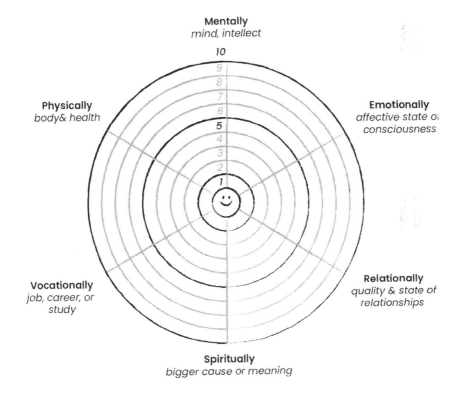

Your Wheel of Life

Let's reflect:

1. How do you feel about the exercise of taking stock of your life?

_____

_____

_____

_____

_____

_____

_____

_____

_____

_____

2. Are you surprised by any of the ratings you gave yourself? Why?

_____

_____

_____

_____

_____

_____

_____

_____

_____

_____

_____

3. Are there any dimensions that you are committed to improving? Which ones? Why?

Articulating Your Core Values

Values are principles, beliefs, or qualities that we consider to be important and worth pursuing. These values can be ethical, professional, cultural, spiritual, or personal. Among the values that we hold dear, usually exists a set of what we call "Core Values." These are essential and central to who we are. Identifying and articulating these core values will bring us closer to knowing ourselves. Behaving in a way that is congruent with our Core Values provides a sense of fulfilment. In this section, we will use an exercise described by TapRoot, at taproot.com, to discover our Core Values.

Let's work:

1. Go through the list of the words representing the different values below and select every word that resonates with you by underlining it, circling it, or highlighting it. Don't overthink your selections, trust your first impressions and don't judge yourself. If you think of a value you possess that is not on the list, be sure to write it down as well (you can add any additional values in the space provided at the end of the last list). There is no upper limit to the number of values you can select, just make sure that you choose at least 20 values.

Abundance
Acceptance
Accountability
Achievement
Adaptability
Adventure
Advocacy
Affection
Ambition
Appreciation
Authenticity
Autonomy
Awareness **A**

Balance
Beauty
Belonging
Benevolence
Boldness
Brilliance **B**

Calmness
Caring
Celebration
Challenge
Change
Charity
Cheerfulness
Clarity
Cleverness
Collaboration
Commitment
Communication
Community **C**

Connection
Consistency
Contentment
Contribution
Curiosity
Cooperation
Courage
Creativity
Credibility
Curiosity **C**

Decisiveness
Dedication
Dependability
Determination
Devotion
Discipline
Diversity **D**

Empathy
Empowerment
Encouragement
Enthusiasm
Equality
Equity
Ethics
Excellence
Expressiveness **E**

Fairness
Faith
Family
Flexibility
Focus **F**

Forgiveness
Freedom
Friendship
Fun **F**

Generosity
Grace
Gratitude
Growth **G**

Happiness
Harmony
Health
Honesty
Hope
Humility
Humour **H**

Impact
Inclusivity
Independence
Individuality
Innovation
Inspiration
Integrity
Intelligence
Intimacy
Intuition **I**

Joy
Justice **J**

Kindness
Knowledge **K**

Leadership
Learning
Love
Loyalty   **L**

Mindfulness
Motivation   **M**

Nature
Neatness
Neutrality   **N**

Open-mindedness
Optimism
Originality   **O**

Patience
Passion
Peace
Perfection
Performance
Perseverance
Personal growth
Playfulness
Positivity
Power
Preparedness
Proactivity
Professionalism
Punctuality
Purpose   **P**

Quality   **Q**

Recognition
Reflection
Relationships
Reliability
Resilience
Resourcefulness
Respect
Responsibility
Responsiveness
Rigour
Risk-taking   **R**

Safety
Security
Self-care
Self-discipline
Self-expression
Selflessness
Self-love
Service
Simplicity
Sincerity
Solitude
Spirituality
Stability
Status
Success
Support
Sustainability   **S**

Teamwork
Thankfulness
Thoughtfulness
Timeliness   **T**

Tolerance
Traditionalism
Trust
Truth   **T**

Understanding
Unity
Uniqueness
Usefulness   **U**

Versatility
Vision
Vitality   **V**

Warmth
Wealth
Wellbeing
Winning
Wisdom
Wonder
Work ethic
Worthiness   **W**

Youthfulness   **Y**

Zeal
Zen   **Z**

Note: Add any missing values below

2. Create 5 categories of the values you selected in the previous exercise by putting those values you feel are similar or have things in common together in the boxes provided. The number of values in each group needs not be the same. If you have more than five groupings, drop those you think are least important. There is no right or wrong way to categorise the values, trust your instinct.

3. Choose one value from each group that best represents the list and can stand as a label for the entire group. Again, do not overthink your choices of labels. These chosen labels represent your Core Values or are very close to being your Core Values.

See the example below.

Let's work:

Now, you do the same, categorise the values you selected in 5 lists and write them in the boxes below. Select a label from each list.

4. Bring your Core Values to life and activate them by adding a verb to each value so you can see what it looks like as an actionable Core Value, for example for the **5 core values** identified earlier we can use:

1. *Uphold Excellence*

2. *Deliver Impact*

3. *Nurture Happiness*

4. *Mobilise Purpose*

5. *Inspire a Common Vision*

Being aware of your Core Values through the exercises of identifying and activating them can provide you with an insight that will help you as you choose the actions you need to take to truly live on purpose.

Now write your activated Core Values below.

1. _____

2. _____

3. _____

4. _____

5. _____

Frequently Asked Questions: [?]

Question 1: Are Core Values stable constructs or do they change as we go through our life journey?

Answer: Core Values usually have stability and endurance to them. However, people do evolve and change particularly if they are exposed to life-altering experiences.

Question 2: If I were to repeat the same Core Values exercise above in a few months, most likely I would not be choosing the exact same words from the lists provided and may end with different Core Values, does that mean I have changed? Does this exercise remain valid?

Answer: You can try repeating the exercise in the future. Chances are you will be choosing similar words and ending with similar Core Values. Remember, we can describe ourselves and our Core Values with different words, but that does not mean we are different. The saying goes that the map is not the territory, similarly, the description is not the item being described.

Question 3: Why did we go through an elimination exercise to identify our Core Values? Can't we just articulate them directly?

Answer: When asked to enumerate their Core Values directly, people may unconsciously feel that they need to select the "right" values and many end up listing those related to integrity, family, and the like. The elimination exercise above is designed to neutralise this bias and help us reach as closely as we can to our authentic values.

Let's reflect:

1. How do you feel about the exercise of discovering and articulating your Core Values?

2. Are you surprised by any of the Core Values you ended up with? Elaborate below.

_____
_____
_____
_____
_____
_____
_____
_____
_____
_____
_____

3. Do these Core Values reflect who you truly are? Elaborate below.

_____
_____
_____
_____
_____
_____
_____
_____
_____
_____
_____
_____
_____
_____
_____

Your Life Journey

Socrates famously said, "The unexamined life is not worth living," a sentiment that resonates through the corridors of philosophy and psychology alike, as scholars and psychotherapists concur on the significance of introspection. The contemplative endeavour of venturing into the corners of our existence, not only facilitates a deeper understanding of oneself but also imbues life's myriad events with a profound sense of meaning and wonder.

In this section, you will explore your life journey and how you shaped the Peak Moments in your life and how they, in turn, shaped you. In the space provided below (feel free to use additional pages) draw your life-line as shown in the example and mark your Peak Moments. These are meaningful events and situations that stood out and shaped you because you were at your best, happiest, proudest, or even most challenged or disappointed.

For each Peak Moment you identify, write:

> *What was happening?*
> *Who you were with?*
> *What values were you honouring (or not honouring)?*
> *What emotions and feelings did you have?*
> *What opportunities did the situation bring?*
> *What lessons did you learn from this moment?*

It is important to make sure you choose Moments and avoid choosing extended periods of time (e.g., my high school years). If you feel that a period is special, attempt to pick the Moment(s) that stood out for you within that period.

An example of a Life-Line and Peak Moments is shown next for your reference. The reflections on the Peak Moments are provided too.

Peak Moments Examples (Your Life-Line)

Age 6
- Won my first Chess competition.
- **Who you were with:** My Mother
- **Values:** Excellence, Discipline, Winning.
- **Feelings & Emotions:** Surprise, Pride, Happiness.
- **Opportunities:** Meeting people with similar interest.
- **Lessons:** I can excel at the things that I enjoy.

Age 12
- Being bullied at school.
- **Who you were with:** My Mother, Teacher, Friends.
- **Values:** Justice, Forgiveness.
- **Feelings & Emotions:** Fear, Disappointment, Lack of Safety.
- **Opportunities:** Building resilience and helping others.
- **Lessons:** I can be strong and there are people to reach out to for help.

Birth (Age)

Age 13
- Running for Student's Union President (and failing).
- **Who you were with:** My Mother, Friends.
- **Values:** Excellence, Resilience, Acceptance.
- **Feelings & Emotions:** Stress, Excitement
- **Opportunities:** Realising the importance of clear communication
- **Lessons:** Failure can be a better teacher than success.

Age 18

- Getting my driver's license and being involved in a car accident.
- **Who you were with:** My Mother Family, Friends.
- **Values:** Resilience, Growth, Endurance.
- **Feelings & Emotions:** Pain, Love, Support.
- **Opportunities:** Reflecting on life and interdependence
- **Lessons:** Realising the importance of health and independence.

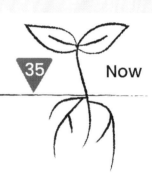

 18   22   35   Now

Age 22

- Loosing mother to cancer.
- **Who you were with:** My Family, Friends.
- **Values:** Resilience, Courage, Patience.
- **Feelings & Emotions:** Loss, Confusion, Pain, Sadness.
- **Opportunities:** Connecting with family members and friends.
- **Lessons:** There will be a day when my mother's memory will bring me joy, not pain.

Age 35

- Completing my PhD.
- **Who you were with:** My Fiancée, Supervisor, Friends.
- **Values:** Excellence, Innovation, Impact, Success.
- **Feelings & Emotions:** Achievement, Happiness, Pride.
- **Opportunities:** Career advancement and mobilising research into real world solutions.
- **Lessons:** Hard work and persistence pay off.

1. What are the repeating or missing themes in your Peak Moments?

The themes of pursuing excellence and overcoming adversity appear to recur throughout my peak moments. They seem to shape my life experiences and define who I am today. Family and friends also feature prominently, aligning with my expectations, given the importance of family and connections with loved ones in my life.

What surprises me, though, is that none of my peak moments are associated with money or financial gain. While I always thought money was a key motivator, reflection has led me to understand that what truly drives me is the ability to deliver high-quality work, which can be associated with financial rewards. Thus, I now view money more as a means to security rather than an end in itself.

2. Are there any specific values that seem to be associated with your Peak Moments? What are these values? Are they similar or different to the Core Values you identified earlier?

Values associated with strength and high performance such as courage, resilience, endurance, patience, and forgiveness (strength values) and excellence, impact, innovation, success, and winning (high-performance values) appear to dominate my peak moments. These are very aligned with the values I identified in my core values exercise.

3. How does remembering your life journey make you feel?

Reflecting on my life journey made me feel grateful for all the people and circumstances who shaped who I am today. Finding alignment between my core values and the values that I upheld during my peak moments gave me further assurance that I am on the right track in my self-development journey.

Remembering my mother and feeling my heart filled with joy as I appreciated all the support and warmth that she brought to my life was a truly special moment.

4. Are there any discoveries and/or surprises at the end of the exercise?

The absence of financial gain as a key driver for me was a surprise and a very helpful discovery. With this deeper self-knowledge, I believe that I can motivate myself even better now.

Let's work:

Now it's your turn. Draw and label your peak moments on your Life -Line.

Birth (Age)

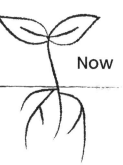

Now

Feel free to use a suitable length for your Life-Line that you can draw on the next pages.

Let's reflect:

1. Are there any repeating or missing themes in your Peak Moments? Is there a common theme or a golden thread that is repeated through more than one Peak Moment? You may notice, for example, that themes such as performance, family, nature, or helping others are repeating through different Peak Moments. You may also observe that some themes that you expected to have are missing. Use the space below to write down your reflections.

2. Are there any specific values that seem to be associated with your Peak Moments? What are these values? Are they similar or different to the Core Values you identified earlier?

3. How does remembering your life journey make you feel?

4. Are there any discoveries and/or surprises at the end of the exercise?

Your "I am" Statement

After all that you have learnt about yourself in the previous exercises, particularly while recalling your Peak Moments when you lived your Core Values and made a positive difference in the lives of others, you are now ready to write your "I am" Statement. The noun in this statement can refer to a trait, an emotion, a feeling, a capability, a capacity, or a quality. When writing your "I am" Statement, you will need to be explorative and avoid generic terms or statements that are defined by your current job, position, or relationship status such as I am an engineer, I am a leader, I am a student, or I am a wife. Your "I am" Statement should describe a key attribute that you possess or manifest, or that you are committed to developing. Think of the "I am" Statement as one describing your **superpower.**

Sometimes, the challenge in selecting an "I am" Statement arises from the concern that opting for a particular word might restrict the ways we articulate our interaction with life or overlook other potential aspects. However, this is not the case. Each of us encompasses various roles and interacts with others and life in diverse ways. Personally, I identify as a storyteller, yet I also fulfil roles as a father, son, husband, engineer, leader, academic, author, and many more. Nevertheless, I sense that storytelling is a distinctive way in which I manifest in all my roles.

There are multiple approaches you can use to uncover and articulate your superpower including self-reflection (by you) and external reflection (by asking others), ideally doing both and experiencing some convergence.

As an exercise in self-reflection, let us examine an example of an internal dialogue that you can have with yourself to elucidate your "I am" Statement. Say, based on your self-exploration, you think that your superpower is your capability to enable teams to face adversity and reach their goals transforming challenges into opportunities, ask the question "How do I achieve this?" repeatedly until you find the unique angle you use to deliver your contribution. See the sample dialogue below:

Question: What is my superpower?

Answer: I enable teams to face adversity and reach their goals transforming challenges into opportunities.

Question : How do I achieve this?

Answer: I help the team members realise that they have a potential that is bigger than the challenge they encounter.

Question: How do I achieve this?

*Answer: I help the team identify pathways to go around the obstacles and reach their goal. **I am a Pathfinder.***

or

*Answer: I help the team see the situation from a different angle, realising some unique positive opportunities. **I am a Perspective Shifter.***

or

*Answer: I help the team by bringing their opposing points of view closer to each other so that they can pull together and go through the difficult time. **I am a Consensus Builder.***

You noticed that there were 3 versions of the answer to the last question. These answers were given by 3 different individuals after they managed to dig deep enough to shed light on the distinctive pathways they use to deliver their unique contribution and guide the formation of their "I am" Statement. While the 3 started by stating that their superpower was to help teams transform adversities into opportunities, through repeated questioning, they eventually realised that their true strengths are in: finding new ways, shifting perspectives, and building consensus, respectively. As a coach, I helped these individuals by asking them to imagine the challenges faced by the team as an obstacle field and think of how they plan to go through it. Some people will find a path within the obstacles (pathfinders), others will think of the obstacles as stepping stones towards different realities (perspective shifters), while some will align the team's strengths to plough through the obstacle field (consensus builders).

Asking others who know you best, as a relative, friend, or co-worker, about which of your qualities and capabilities they miss the most when you are not present can be quite revealing and eye-opening. Following up with a question about their recollection of times when they saw you at your best, can help you see your superpower through the eyes of others.

Sometimes, the easiest way to find your "I am" Statement is to look at what you hate or do not like and use the positive opposite to frame the "I am" Statement. For Example:

▶ I hate fake. **I am an Authenticity-Enabler.**

▶ I hate conflict. **I am a Peacemaker.**

▶ I hate betrayal. **I am a Loyalty-Advocate.**

Below are examples of good "I am" Statements that can inspire you:

▶ I am an authenticity-enabler.

▶ I am a bridge-builder.

▶ I am a builder of relationships.

▶ I am a catalyst.

▶ I am a change-maker.

▶ I am a cheerleader.

▶ I am a coalition-builder.

▶ I am a connector.

▶ I am a consensus-maker.

▶ I am a creator of hope.

► I am a curator of serendipity.

► I am a difference-maker.

► I am a dot connector.

► I am a dream-catcher.

► I am a driver of change.

► I am an enabler.

► I am an energiser.

► I am an explorer.

► I am a force-multiplier.

► I am a game-changer.

► I am a giver.

► I am an initiator.

► I am a life-giver.

► I am a loyalty-enabler.

► I am a mathmagician.

► I am a myth-buster.

► I am a nation-builder.

► I am a negotiator.

► I am a nurturer.

► I am an optimist.

► I am an organiser.

► I am a paradigm-shifter.

► I am a pathfinder.

► I am a pattern-finder.

► I am a peacemaker.

► I am a peacekeeper.

► I am a perspective-shifter.

► I am a prime-mover.

► I am a protector.

► I am a risk-mitigator.

► I am a seed-planter.

► I am a silver lining.

► I am a simplifier.

► I am a solution-finder.

► I am a soul-warrior.

► I am a storyteller.

► I am a strategic thinker.

► I am a strength-multiplier.

► I am a trust-builder.

► I am a value-creator.

Let's review: ✓

Let us do some final checks on your "I am" Statement:

1. **Your "I am" Statement describes your superpower.** Consider writing it in positive, affirmative, and specific language.

2. **Remember, selecting an "I am" Statement does not exclude the myriad of other ways we show up in life.** On the contrary, it enhances the authenticity and distinctiveness with which we manifest our presence and deliver our impact.

3. **While being poetic is good, your "I am" Statement should be understandable without much explanation and can stand on its own in a professional setting.** For example, one of my students came up with "I am a washing machine" as his statement. Upon discussion, we realised that he was referring to his ability to deal with difficult situations and transform them into fresh opportunities. After brainstorming, the student saw fit that he would change his statement to "I am an agent of transformation."

Next is a diagrammatic representation of the process of finding the "I am" Statement.

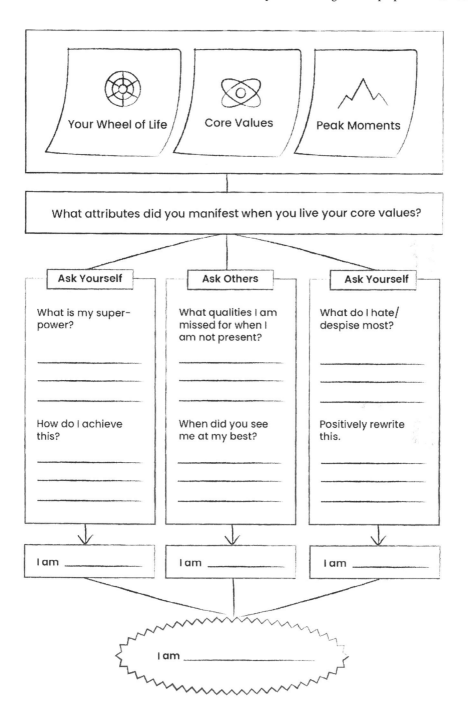

Finding Your "I Am" Statement

Now you are ready to write down your "I am" Statement. Don't worry, many of us tweak and change the "I am" Statement as we go through the exercise. Just trust the process. You will be able to revisit this later. Write your "I am" Statement in the box below:

> I am _____

Let's reflect:

1. Share your Core Values and "I am" Statement with 5 friends and/or family members and seek their feedback. Ask them:

   ▶ *What are their thoughts about your commitment to articulating your superpower?*

   ▶ *Do your Core Values describe you well?*

   ▶ *Is your "I am" Statement reflective of the qualities and capabilities that they recognise you for?*

   ▶ *Do they have any alternative suggestions?*

Outline the essence of these conversations below.

2. How do you feel about performing and completing the exercise of articulating your "I am" Statement?

3. Are there any discoveries and/or surprises at the end of this exercise?

4

Discovering Your Purpose

"Purpose is a stable and generalised intention to accomplish something that is at once meaningful to the self and consequential to the world beyond the self."

-William Damon

One of the key differentiating features between humans and animals is the fact that animals' behaviour and conduct are, to a large extent, driven by reflex and instinct. Ants will always collaborate to collect and store food, bees will always make honey, and mice will always fall for the cheese inside a mouse trap.

Humans are much more sophisticated and individualistic and have huge potential for learning, creation, and impact. While we do have basic instincts such as survival, avoiding pain, and seeking pleasure, these instincts are not sufficient to drive or even comprehensively explain human behaviour. Another differentiator is that humans are aware of their mortality. Without something deeper and more meaningful at the personal level to make life worth living, we can experience boredom and hopelessness and our wellbeing may suffer.

In the absence of a true purpose, people may seek—consciously or unconsciously—alternative sources of meaning to fill the void. We all read about and have witnessed political leaders inspiring the masses to what may be less-than-ideal actions. The level of conviction and the willingness to sacrifice by the members of these groups, in the interest of a false cause, is evidence that they believe in and even draw a sense of meaning from it.

There are two types of purpose; true purpose, which is innately good, emanates from within, and generally has a positive impact on the world, and false purpose, which is usually manipulated, is often driven from outside (the latest fads, being part of a group), and does not have a positive impact on the world. The former requires intentional work and discipline to discover and mobilise, and it is the focus of this book, while the latter can exist without much intentional effort.

The true purpose is the desire to work on something meaningful that transcends one's self. William Damon[1], a Stanford University professor, defines purpose as "a stable and generalised intention to accomplish something that is at once meaningful to the self and consequential to the world beyond the self." As we mentioned earlier, a growing body of research is pointing towards developing a sense of purpose as a prerequisite for good mental health, success, and happiness. A clear sense of purpose, however, is not something that will appear spontaneously and often requires structured work and intentional effort to uncover and develop it, hence this book.

Purpose can, but need not, be heroic or larger than life. Purpose-driven people can, for example, draw a huge sense of satisfaction from their work and service to others regardless of the size of the services and the jobs they perform or the status that comes with them.

Purpose-driven individuals engage in work that is necessary for others, enjoyable, aligned with their skills, and often financially rewarding. This concept is illustrated by the Japanese principle of ikigai, as depicted in the Venn diagram below. In the Japanese language, ikigai translates to "reason for being," with "iki" signifying "life" and "kai" connoting "meaning or results." Ikigai encapsulates the idea of having a meaningful direction or a sense of purpose in life. Psychologist Michiko Kumano describes it as "entailing actions of devoting oneself to pursuits one enjoys and is associated with feelings of accomplishment and fulfilment."

Research done on a sample of 510 undergraduate students at Heriot-Watt University Malaysia demonstrated the benefit of defining ikigai since students reported they had learned key skills in self-leadership.

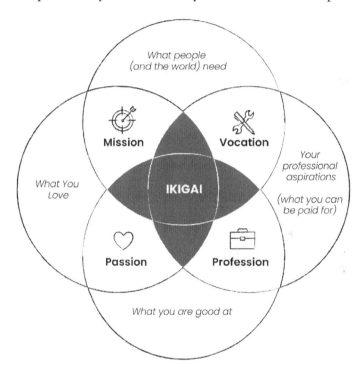

Discovering Your Purpose (Ikigai)

Reverse Engineering Your Ikigai

In this chapter, we are going to reverse engineer your ikigai by creating 4 lists for the 4 circles of the above diagram and looking for areas of commonality and intersection that can direct you towards discovering what your purpose is.

Let's work:

1. Create a list of the world's needs that you feel passionate about or a list of the characteristics of your ideal world. For example, you may think that the world needs more self-awareness, justice, environmental protection, or economic opportunities. Items on this list could be things that people in your city or community, or indeed the whole world, need. For inspiration with regard to the big needs of the world, you can refer to the United Nations Sustainable Development Goals. For example, you might be passionate about climate action, poverty, education, or life below water.

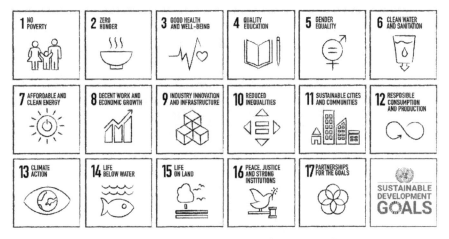

United Nations Sustainable Development Goals

List 10 of the world needs that you are passionate about below:

2. Now create a list of your strengths and the things that you are good at. These can be:

► *Internal qualities you possess such as the ability to remain calm under pressure, introspection, critical thinking, creativity, resilience, and patience.*

► *Capabilities to effectively work and interact with other people, such as negotiation, sales, teaching, listening, empathy, or leadership.*

► *Skills to work with things such as playing music, carving wood, writing, cooking, working with large sets of data, or editing videos.*

Remember, you do not have to be the best in the world at something to consider it a strength. If others consistently seek your help in certain areas, this is a good indication that you are good at that.

Now list down 10 things that you are good at, and others recognise you for, below:

3. Enumerate the things that genuinely resonate with you and bring you joy. This should be a straightforward exercise. In order to discern potential patterns that point toward your purpose, feel free to include items that occurred in the lists created earlier. Be detailed and specific; for instance, if you expressed a love for food, elaborate on what aspects of food captivate you. It could be the exploration of diverse cultures through their cuisine or the joy of connecting with people over shared meals. Similarly, if watching TV is an interest, specify the particular shows that you find appealing. For example, you might enjoy historical documentaries as a way of engaging with this form of entertainment.

List 10 things that you love and love doing below:

4. The fourth list delineates your career and professional aspirations, focusing on how you can derive value, earn a livelihood, and contribute to the professional growth of others while pursuing your purpose. This list will vary significantly based on your current life stage, career trajectory, and individual needs. As examples, you might include aspirations such as securing a promotion, launching a business, attaining a CEO position, or participating in and leading professional associations.

Please write your list below. Try to have 10 items on this list too.

Now, look for **common themes and areas** in the 4 lists you created. If at first glance no common themes seem to emerge, do not despair, this is normal. Re-examine the items on your lists and try to sharpen and nuance them further as mentioned earlier. For example, if you wrote "playing computer games" in the "what you love list," try to ask yourself what you love about computer games. You may then realise that you love the challenge of the game, or you enjoy connecting and competing with other people. Below is an example:

The World Needs

1. Fair wages
2. Equality
3. Access to education
4. Youth empowerment
5. Employability
6. Peace
7. Harmony
8. Economic opportunities
9. Sustainable growth
10. Renewable energy

I'd Like to be Paid For

1. Leading as a CEO
2. Teaching math
3. Building stuff
4. Teaching/training
5. Public speaking
6. Empowering others
7. Travelling
8. Supporting the youth
9. Being a business owner
10. Tasting food

IKIGAI

I Love

1. Music
2. Reading
3. Travelling
4. Meeting others
5. Challenging
6. Public speaking
7. Art
8. Travelling
9. Good food
10. Being with friends

I'm Good At

1. Organising
2. Writing
3. Self-awareness
4. Explaining concepts
5. Technology
6. Debating
7. Public speaking
8. Building partnerships
9. Handiwork
10. Gardening

After completing the 4 lists above, the person undertaking the work can:

1. *Examine the above 4 lists carefully looking for common themes.* *In this case, there are several common themes. These include the youth, fairness, jobs, and economic opportunities.*

2. *Review their Core Values and explore how connected these values are to the common themes* *to gain a deeper understanding of their ikigai.*

3. *Inspect their life journey and Peak Moments through the lens of the common themes* *to discover any links there.*

4. *Speak with family and friends* *who know them well to see how people see them and what they think about their ikigai.*

Taking all of the above into account, the ikigai of this person appears to revolve around helping youth, especially fresh graduates receive fair wages. Their purpose statement is:

My purpose is to promote fair wages for the youth.

Now it is your turn to discover your purpose.

Let's work:

1. Fill in the 4 lists below and reflect on what is common.

2. What are the common themes emerging for you from your 4 lists above? Write them down below.

3. Review your Core Values and explore how connected these values are to your common themes.

    ▶ *How do your Core Values connect with your strengths?*

    ▶ *How do your Core Values connect with what you love doing?*

    ▶ *How do your Core Values connect with what the world needs?*

    ▶ *How do your Core Values connect with the kind of work you wish to do for a living?*

    Comment on the connections (or the lack thereof) below.

_____

_____

_____

_____

_____

_____

_____

_____

_____

_____

_____

_____

_____

_____

_____

_____

_____

_____

_____

_____

_____

4. Inspect your life journey and Peak Moments through the lens of the common themes of your ikigai. Are there any connections?

   ▶ *Do you think that your strengths and capabilities were built or enhanced by your life experiences? How?*

   ▶ *Do your Peak Moments occur when you are doing what you love doing and/or what you are good at?*

   ▶ *Do the world's needs (or the needs of others) influence your life journey or your Peak Moments? How?*

   ▶ *How did the kind of work you wish to do for a living feature in your life thus far? Do you think you have sufficient opportunities to do the work you wish to do?*

Outline your answers, reflections, and any interesting findings below.

5. Feel free to share what you have discovered with people who know
    you best and seek their advice. If you spoke to people, write below the
    key reflection points.

Finally, reflecting on your ikigai and the exercises you have done thus far, how would you describe your purpose? Below are some examples to inspire you.

▶ **I am a storyteller.** My purpose is to inspire others to tell more empowering stories about themselves and the world we live in.

▶ **I am a simplifier.** My purpose is to promote harmony by championing plain language.

▶ **I am a value creator.** My purpose is to translate socio-environmental complexities into sustainable opportunities.

▶ **I am a math lover.** My purpose is to use my mastery of mathematics to reduce complexity for others when they need it the most.

▶ **I am a difference maker.** My purpose is to create a world where role models are judged by their compassion and dedication.

▶ **I am a builder of relationships.** My purpose is to use the trust that I develop to help create employment opportunities for others.

▶ **I am a self-explorer.** My purpose is to organise the world so that vital food resources aren't needlessly wasted.

▶ **I am an authenticity enabler.** My purpose is to help people find their inner voice and gift that to the world.

▶ **I am a vehicle for change.** My purpose is to drive social justice for voiceless communities.

▶ **I am an advocate.** My purpose is to inspire and empower mental health literacy and acceptance through holistic mental health policy change.

▶ **I am a connector.** My purpose is to use graphic design to help people and brands connect with their inner magic and gift it to the world.

► **I am a driver of change.** My purpose is to bring enjoyment and security of life to others by creating a globally sustainable society.

► **I am an optimist.** My purpose is to turn uncertainties into opportunities, helping many realise their financial freedom by optimising these opportunities.

► **I am a nurturer.** My purpose is to use my life experience to inspire others, particularly women, to believe in themselves and their potential.

Let's review: ☑

Let us do some final checks on your purpose statement:

1. **Consider writing your purpose in positive language.** When Mother Teresa was invited to support an anti-war rally she said I do not go to "anti" rallies, when you have a pro-peace rally, call me. Likewise if, for example, your purpose is "fighting disease," consider transforming it to "promoting health." If it is to "eradicate pollution," consider "championing sustainability."

2. **Purpose is not a goal.** If your purpose sounded like a goal, for example, "to increase customer satisfaction," or "to improve sales" try to go back to your ikigai and repeat the work following the instructions. Ask yourself, why increasing customers' satisfaction or sales is important. Maybe whatever you are selling will help customers succeed in addressing some world needs. That could be an indication of what your purpose is.

3. **True purpose can fit both your personal and professional lives.** If you end up with a Purpose Statement that fits only the personal or the professional aspects of your life, try to explore further and dig deeper to find some common ground.

4. **With your self-knowledge improving as you articulate your purpose, you may feel the need to change your "I am" Statement, this is absolutely fine.** If you feel some update for your "I am" Statement is appropriate, go ahead and make the changes. You may change this again in the future.

When ready, write your "I am" Statement and Purpose Statement in the box provided:

I am

My purpose is

Frequently Asked Questions:

Question 1: Am I too young or too old to articulate my purpose?

Answer: It is never too early or too late to start discovering and articulating your true purpose. Now, more than ever, this is becoming a fundamental need. Formulating your purpose is a necessity, not a luxury.

Question 2: Will articulating a well-defined purpose prevent me from exploring other things in life?

Answer: On the contrary, the true purpose is an enabler, not an inhibitor. Expressing and declaring your purpose will also send a signal to those of similar interest to join you and collaborate with you.

Question 3: Should purpose be heroic or larger than life?

Answer: Not necessarily. Your true purpose can be as large or as focused as it suits you.

Question 4: Will my purpose change as I go through life?

Answer: While true purpose possesses inherent stability, the manner in which you articulate your purpose will naturally evolve over time as your self-knowledge matures and deepens. Similar to the phenomenon of perceiving something from a distance versus up close, our descriptions may vary as we gain a clearer and more intimate understanding of ourselves.

Question 5: Can my purpose be framed in an aspirational way, or should it be something that I already have?

Answer: Purpose can be conceptualised through the ideals we aspire to pursue, aspirational true purpose can encourage us to live up to its higher standards.

Question 6: Will I one day just discover my true purpose spontaneously? Or is intentional work necessary?

Answer: It is necessary to intentionally work on discovering and committing to paper your true purpose. A structured impact statement workshop, under the tutelage of an experienced impact coach, is a very effective way to achieve that. The next best thing is to complete this workbook.

Let's reflect:

1. Share your Purpose Statement with at least 5 friends and/or family members and seek their feedback. What are their thoughts? Does your purpose describe you well? Do they have any alternative suggestions?

2. How do you feel about the exercise of articulating your purpose?

3. How does your "I am" Statement connect with your Purpose Statement? Is there a natural flow between the two?

_____
_____
_____
_____
_____
_____
_____
_____
_____
_____
_____

4. Are there any discoveries and/or surprises?

_____
_____
_____
_____
_____
_____
_____
_____
_____
_____
_____
_____
_____
_____

5

Mobilising Your Purpose into a Positive Impact

"The purpose of human life is to serve, and to show compassion and the will to help others."

-Albert Schweitzer

After articulating your "I am" Statement and Purpose Statement, it is essential that you use the momentum to mobilise your purpose into a positive impact on the world. In this chapter, you will formulate your Actions Statement which will describe your overall strategy to mobilise your purpose. But first, you will practice setting some goals that you wish to achieve on the way to bringing your purpose to flourishing. This is an opportunity to align the goals describing whatever you want to achieve in your studies, career, personal growth, or service to your purpose. You will set a goal that you would like to accomplish in the next 12 months, and another goal to deliver in the next 36 months. Thinking of your goals will help you direct, focus, and sharpen your Actions Statement. The goals you will set need to be S.M.A.R.T., so let us briefly explore the concept of S.M.A.R.T. goals.

S.M.A.R.T. Goals

Planning and goal-setting are crucial activities for individuals and organisations to realise their mission and vision, bringing their purpose to fruition. While purpose mobilisation is a lifelong endeavour, goals must be established and accomplished within a more foreseeable timeframe. To guarantee the achievement of goals contributing to mission fulfilment, it's imperative that goals be Specific, Measurable, Attainable, Relevant, and Time-bound. Below is a brief review of each aspect of S.M.A.R.T. goals.

Specific Goals

A specific goal is clear and not ambiguous. It needs to indicate who is involved in achieving it, what needs to be accomplished, where it will take place, when it will happen and how it will be achieved. For example, "to get in shape" is rather a general goal, while "develop a programme of diet and exercise under the supervision of a coach" is a specific goal.

Measurable Goals

Here, we need to specify the metrics for measuring the goal so that we can unambiguously know when the goal is achieved. For example, "increase sales" is not measurable, while "increase sales by 10% compared to last year" is measurable.

Attainable Goals

For goals to be attainable, there should be no natural, ethical, or legal barrier against them. When setting goals, one must also acknowledge environmental and physical limitations. For goals to motivate, they need to represent a stretch on what is perceived as being possible while simultaneously ensuring that the skills, capabilities and attitudes that make the goals attainable are within the reach of those who are working towards them. For example, if I do not know how to swim now, setting a goal of winning an Olympic medal in 6 months is unattainable and will demotivate me as I go about my weekly training. However, the goal of qualifying for a local swimming competition within a year is very motivating; even though it stretches me, if I train long enough, I have a very good shot at achieving it.

Relevant Goals

The goals we set should be relevant and congruent with the overall Purpose Statement developed earlier. A football coach, for example, may set the goal of "making two egg sandwiches by 9 a.m." The goal is specific, measurable, attainable and time-bound, but it is hardly relevant if the overall objective is to increase the tactical skills of the team. Relevant goals are worthwhile; they add real value and capitalise on the strengths and capabilities of the team members.

Time-Bound Goals

The goals need to have clear timelines indicating when they will be achieved.

While setting S.M.A.R.T. goals is a very important activity, it is essential here to remain flexible, agile and open to review the goals should an attractive unforeseen opportunity arise or when the internal or external environments change. If we work in the mining business and while digging for silver, we find gold; we should have the mental agility to change our goals to capture the new "golden" opportunity.

When I worked on my PhD research, my project focused on exploring the relationship between fluid mechanics and the formation of gallstones in the gallbladder. The work involved building models of the cystic ducts of patients who underwent surgical removal of the gallbladder and studying the flow inside them. While observing the flow structures, I noticed that there was some fluid mixing occurring within the cystic duct that connects the gallbladder to the rest of the biliary system. While, strictly speaking, my S.M.A.R.T. goal was to explore the relationship between gallstones and the mechanics of the flow, I opted to pursue the mixing opportunity as a viable industrial option. This ended up being a significant part of my doctoral work and even influenced the title of my thesis, which I changed to *"Cystic Duct to Static Mixer: A Serendipitous Journey."*

Let me reiterate: setting S.M.A.R.T. goals is crucial for successful planning. However, maintaining an open mind and preserving intellectual agility allows us to adjust the S.M.A.R.T. goals to yield the best outcome should there be a change that was not foreseen when the goal was set. When we change and update our S.M.A.R.T. goals, it is necessary that we communicate the change and its reasons to other team members and also document the change process adequately.

Now, think of two S.M.A.R.T. goals that can bring you closer to mobilising your purpose into a positive impact on others, one goal is to be completed within the next 12 months and the other within the next 36 months. As mentioned earlier, these goals can be aligned with your studies or career objectives, spiritual or professional development, or the volunteering and service you would like to be involved with. Articulate these two goals in the table below as shown in the example.

You may need more work space or you may be inspired to have more **S.M.A.R.T. goals**, feel free to add those in the space available below or on external additional pages.

	Specific	Measurable	Attainable	Relevant	Time-Bound
Description	What do you want to accomplish? Who needs to be included?	How to measure progress & know that you have achieved your goal?	What skills, resources, and networks do you need to achieve your goal?	How relevant is this to your purpose?	When will this goal be achieved?
Example	Improve mathematics for children by running technology based workshops.	Traning 1000 children aged 10-15 years so that they can pass mathematics standard test.	1. Organisational skills. 2. Collaboration with NGOs. 3. Attracting volunteers.	My purpose is to enable children to achieve their full potential through mastering mathematics.	12 months from the start date of the project.
	Now it's your turn! Fill in the blank with your goals				
12 Months Goal					
36 Months Goal					

Your S.M.A.R.T Goals

Actions Statement

The final part of your Impact Statement is the Actions Statement that outlines your strategy and your commitment to realising your purpose. This will take into account everything that you have explored, reflected on and, discovered about yourself thus far. Your Actions Statement will describe how you will leverage your strengths, relationships, networks, and resources to build coalitions and find pathways to help overcome the obstacles on your pathways to realising your purpose.

Let's work:

1. Who are the people and communities you care for and wish to positively impact?

2. What communities and networks do you have close links with that can help you mobilise your purpose?

3. What are the key obstacles, personal or external, that may prevent you from mobilising your purpose?

4. What resources, networks, strengths, and capabilities can you leverage to overcome these obstacles or discover alternative pathways?

Now you can start writing your **Actions Statement** in the format below. Here are two examples to inspire you:

▶ I am a builder of relationships. My purpose is to use the trust that I develop to help create employment opportunities for others. **I am helping the workforce of tomorrow to navigate the 4ᵗʰ Industrial Revolution today.**

▶ I am a storyteller. My purpose is to inspire others to tell empowering stories about themselves and the world we live in. **I dedicate my life to supporting youth to be their best as they identify their impact, harness their talent and become purposeful individuals.**

Let's review: ✓

Sometimes, as we shape our Actions Statement and reflect on what we would like to do to mobilise our purpose, we get inspired to refocus and sharpen our Purpose Statement and even "I am" Statement. This is normal. Write your final statements in the box provided.

I am

My purpose is

I (will/ dedicate my life for/ endeavour to)

CONGRATULATIONS!

This is an amazing achievement that you reached with your dedication and hard work. However, you need to remember that this is just the beginning of a life journey of pursuing your purpose. Your Impact Statement is a powerful tool to communicate who you are to others, once you feel happy with it, you can include it in your CV, share it on social media or even on the back of your business card.

It would also be helpful to assign some of your trusted friends or family members as impact partners and give them the permission to check with you from time to time on how are you getting on with your purpose to impact journey.

Let's reflect:

1. Share your Impact Statement with at least 5 friends and/or family members and seek their feedback. What are their thoughts? Does your Impact Statement suit you and feel empowering and inspiring? Do they have any alternative suggestions?

2. How do you feel about the exercise of articulating your Impact Statement?

3. Are there any discoveries and/or surprises?

Delivering Impact Through Purpose-Driven Education

As mentioned earlier, all students and staff members at my university commence their journey with us by going through an exercise of articulating their Impact Statements. Students undertake this task under the guidance of trained Impact Coaches in the first 4 weeks of the inaugural semester of their undergraduate studies. Subsequently, during the second semester, students who share a common sense of purpose, interests, and aspirations come together to establish Impact Teams, each comprising approximately 10 members. These teams collaborate to launch crowdfunding campaigns with the aim of raising funds for NGOs engaged in social service aligned with the Impact Teams' shared purpose.

Simply Giving Crowdfunding Page
(source: https://www.simplygiving.com/event/hw-empower-2023)

Students set ambitious Impact Targets and frequently meet and surpass them. This exercise not only enhances students' entrepreneurial skills but also fosters increased self-confidence in their capacity to translate their purpose into tangible impact, thereby making a difference in the lives of others. In the year 2023, students collectively set an Impact Target of raising 100,000 Malaysian Ringgit and exceeded this goal.

Crowdfunding is a unique method of raising funds and creating enduring impact as it requires activating the students' networks, leveraging social capital, and reaching out to numerous individuals and organisations through a compelling message. A wide range of NGOs and their supported communities benefited from this work including Teach for Malaysia, MERCY Malaysia, the Malaysian Federation of the Deaf, Green Ribbon Foundation, EPIC Homes, Fugee Schools, and many more. At the end of the campaign, we organise a ceremony for our students to present mock cheques for the representatives of the supported NGOs. These events become sources of pride and inspiration, encouraging others to believe in their capacity to have an impact and make a difference.

A Year 1 Student Presenting A Cheque to the
Representative of MERCY Malaysia

The work extends beyond collaboration with NGOs to include close interaction with the beneficiary communities they support. This engagement leads to the development of a profound understanding of the challenges faced by these communities and instils empathy among the students. This transformative experience has a lasting positive impact, shaping the students' outlook. Even during job interviews, many of our students frequently reference their involvement in translating their purpose into positive impact as a formative experience in their leadership development.

The work undertaken at Heriot-Watt University is an example of how an educational institution can make the discovery of individual purpose central to the development of graduates who are ready to flourish and positively contribute in a changing world.

6

Crafting A Purpose-Driven Life

"Your living is determined not so much by what life brings to you as by the attitude you bring to life; not so much by what happens to you as by the way your mind looks at what happens."

-Khalil Gibran

When we made the decision that every student and staff member at Heriot-Watt University's campus in Malaysia should commence their journey by discovering their purpose and articulating their Impact Statement, we grappled with a critical question: What if, as a result, many students and colleagues realise they are pursuing the "wrong" programme of study or in the "wrong" job? Despite this potential challenge, we moved forward with our plans, firmly believing that life is too precious to be spent studying programmes or working at jobs that do not align with an individual's purpose. I am pleased to report that, while a few students and even fewer colleagues chose to explore other paths, the majority discovered that affirming their purpose reinforced their academic and professional choices.

The process of articulating an Impact Statement often prompts deep introspection and raises questions about the alignment of one's field of study, current job, or life in general to their declared purpose. Sometimes individuals undertake the action of purpose discovery when standing at a crossroads or feeling stuck, seeking clarity on the best path to invest the rest of their lives.

If, after discovering your purpose and articulating the impact you want to have on the world, you harbour doubts about your current endeavours—whether in studies, work, or life in general—I do not necessarily recommend making abrupt changes. Unless you are certain that the misalignment is irreconcilable and that potentially better options exist, I suggest considering a version of the job crafting exercise described by Amy Wrzesniewski, Justin Berg, and Jane Dutton[1].

Job crafting, which can be extended to other professional and personal domains, is rooted in organisational psychology and it involves proactive and intentional changes people make to their own job roles. The goal is to better align these roles with their purpose, skills, strengths, passions, and values. It empowers individuals to reshape various aspects of their work, fostering increased job satisfaction, engagement, and overall well-being.

Key aspects of job crafting include:

1. **Task Crafting:** Individuals modify the type and scope of their tasks, emphasising activities they find more meaningful or enjoyable.

2. **Relational Crafting:** This involves adjusting the nature and depth of interactions with colleagues, supervisors, or clients to cultivate more positive and fulfilling relationships. This often entails cultivating empathy and open-mindedness to appreciate others' points of view as a precursor to transforming the relationships with them.

3. **Cognitive Crafting:** Individuals reinterpret how they perceive their tasks or responsibilities, framing them in a way that enhances their sense of purpose, impact, and value creation.

Work takes a sizable percentage of our time and it can be a major source of identity and meaning for people, not only a way to make a living. That is why job crafting aims at transforming work by recognising and empowering the unique preferences and strengths of individuals. By actively shaping their roles, employees can create a more personalised and fulfilling work experience, enabling them to take ownership of their professional development and job satisfaction.

In this chapter, I propose a modified life-crafting process to provide an opportunity to explore how our life, work, or field of study can be better aligned with our purpose. This process aims to maximise the chances of mobilising this purpose into a positive impact on the world. The detailed process is described in the following sections.

Task Crafting

Task crafting entails reconfiguring the activities, responsibilities, and duties that we are required to perform and reshaping them in a manner that capitalises on our strengths, enhances our satisfaction, and maximises our impact.

To perform a structured task crafting exercise, follow the steps herewith to complete the task crafting table shown below:

1. *Identify the top 10 tasks integral to your job, study (if you are a student), or other life endeavours you are exploring. If you think you need to list more than 10 tasks, go ahead and do that.*

2. *Approximate the percentage of your time allocated to each of these tasks.*

3. *Recalling your ikigai, reflect on each task through the lenses of how good you are at it, assigning it a Strength Alignment level (Low-Medium-High) and how much you enjoy performing it, assigning it a Level of Enjoyment indicator (Low-Medium-High).*

Refer to the example below, completed by an executive at a multinational corporation—let's call her Sandy.

	Task	Percentage of Time %	Strengths Alignment	Level of Enjoyment
1	Setting and monitoring performance targets	30%	Low	Medium
2	Meeting and influencing regulators and Board Members	20%	High "Communication"	Low
3	Developing and monitoring risk registers	10%	Low	Low
4	Analysing financial statements	10%	Low	Low
5	Raising funds	5%	Medium	Low
6	Monitoring market trends and writing reports	5%	Medium	Medium
7	Communicating the strategy internally and externally	5%	High "Communication"	High
8	Meeting customers	5%	High "Making a Difference"	High
9	Developing team leaders	5%	High "Developing Others"	High
10	Influence product design	5%	High "Innovation"	High

Ideally, we need to be spending most of our time on productive and impactful tasks that enable us to utilise our strengths while drawing a good sense of enjoyment and fulfilment. Examining the above table there are a number of opportunities for task crafting that Sandy can embark on:

1. Sandy can begin by scrutinising each task on her list to ensure its alignment with both her personal purpose and the organisational mission. She should assess whether each task is genuinely vital for her success and the success of the organisation, and if she is allocating the appropriate percentage of her time to each. This initial step in task

crafting aims to confirm that Sandy is engaging in tasks that are not only correct for her role but also that she is dedicating an appropriate amount of time to each of them. If any changes to the tasks and the time allocated to them are necessary, Sandy should start conversing with her line manager and other stakeholders to enable this crucial first step in her task crafting journey to take place.

2. Although setting and monitoring performance targets (task No.1) is a key task, Sandy finds it to be neither aligned with her strengths nor highly enjoyable, she still spends 30% of her time on this task. Conversely, she takes pleasure in developing team leaders (task No. 9) but allocates only 5% of her time to it. Sandy can explore integrating tasks 1 and 9 by enhancing her strengths in goal-setting and performance monitoring processes and transforming them into developmental processes for her direct reports. This may necessitate some cultural change and policy adjustments, but such task crafting has the potential to enhance her job satisfaction and impact.

3. While task No. 2 aligns with Sandy's strengths, it brings her very little enjoyment. As this is a task of high strategic significance, Sandy can consider examining the reasons for the low enjoyment level. This could be an indication that she needs to improve her relationships with the regulators and board members which will be covered in the relationship crafting section.

4. For tasks 3-6, Sandy could work on strengthening her teams' capabilities, enabling them to support her in these activities that may not be in her strengths domain. This approach would allow her to allocate more time where she is most effective and impactful.

5. For tasks 7-10, Sandy can explore ways to maximise her impact if these tasks are crucial for the rest of the organisation.

You can now use a similar approach to perform your own task crafting.

Let's work:

In the table below, fill in the top 10 tasks you spend most of your time working on and assess their alignment with your strengths identified in your ikigai in Chapter 4 (Low-Medium-High) and also your level of enjoyment performing them (Low-Medium-High).

1. Are there any changes to the tasks or the percentage of time spent on your list that you would like to introduce to better mobilise your purpose into a positive impact? What are these changes? How do you plan to realise the change? What obstacles may hinder your ability to enact the change?

	Task	Percentage of Time %	Strengths Alignment	Level of Enjoyment
1				
2				
3				
4				
5				
6				
7				
8				
9				
10				

The Top 10 Tasks You Spend Most of Your Time Performing

2. What tasks can you modify to better align with your strengths and purpose? How do you plan to make these changes?

3. What tasks are currently well-aligned with your strengths and purpose? How can you increase your engagement in these tasks?

Relational Crafting

Cultivating relationships that bolster and enhance your sense of purpose at work, school, or in life is a fundamental aspect of life crafting. Opting to collaborate and connect with individuals who share similar values or engage in projects that contribute to a positive impact on a broader scale will not only enhance our enjoyment of what we do but also expand our overall influence. Building on Robert Waldinger and Marc Schulz's concept of a visual social universe from their book "The Good Life," [2] this section adapts the idea to facilitate relational crafting.

The social, or professional, universe can be visualised using a two-by-two matrix with one axis referring to the frequency of interaction within the relationship and the other to the impact the relationship is having on the sense of purpose, whether energising or depleting. In the example shown below, an individual who is performing relational crafting on their job evaluates the different relationships they have with peers, superiors, and other stakeholders by placing them in the corresponding.

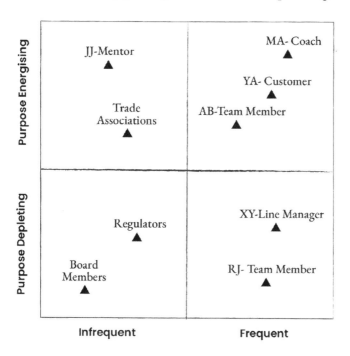

The Visual Social/ Professional Universe

The fabric of the life we lead is woven with the relationships we share. These connections are pivotal to our success, happiness, and the fulfilment of our impact and purpose. We can all identify individuals whose company energises, uplifts, inspires, and encourages us, as well as those we avoid because they drain our energy.

Relational crafting aims to examine all relationships crucial for our success, realising our purpose, and expanding our impact. The goal is to shift as many relationships as possible into the quadrant of purpose-energising and frequent interactions while minimising relationships that deplete our sense of purpose. When seeking to transform and change our relationships, we are often reminded not only to seek change in others but also to be the change we want to see in the world.

Let's work:

1. List the top 10-20 relationships you engage with as part of your work, study, or life requirements. Depending on the domain that you are crafting, these can be relationships with individuals such as superiors, peers, colleagues, and customers, or with groups, departments, and organisations.

2. In the social (professional) universe diagram below, place these top 10-
    20 relationships in the suitable quadrant depending on the frequency
    of interaction and their impact on your purpose.

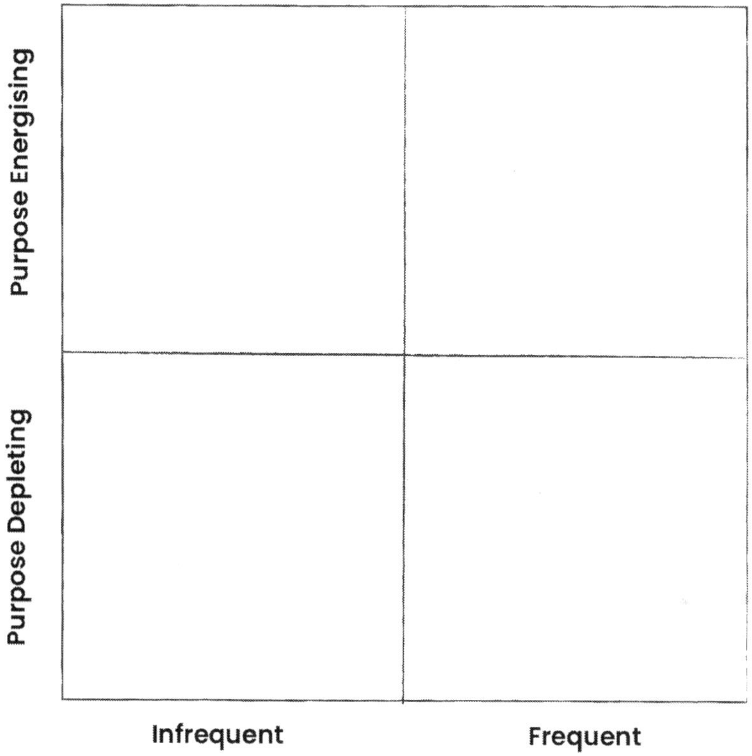

The Visual Social/ Professional Universe

3. Are there any relationships that do not have the potential to contribute to your success or the mobilisation of your purpose into a positive impact on the world? Why are they in your social (professional) universe? Would you like to minimise their presence? How can you achieve that?

4. Are there any relationships necessary for your success and the mobilisation of your purpose that are not in your social (professional) universe? What relationships are these? What plans do you have to bring them into your social (professional) universe?

5. What can you do to move more relationships into the purpose-energising quadrants? Remember, this may require that you change your behaviour, mindset, or perception.

6. What can you do to minimise the purpose-depleting relationships and move them into the infrequent quadrant?

Cognitive Crafting

Cognitive Crafting involves intentionally reshaping how you perceive your role. It goes beyond the surface tasks and encourages a deeper exploration of the meaning and purpose embedded in your contributions. This process entails a deliberate effort to connect your day-to-day responsibilities with your Impact Statement and the broader, positive effect you are having on people and communities beyond yourself. By reframing your perception, you not only find intrinsic motivation in your tasks but also recognise the significance of your role in contributing to meaningful and positive outcomes on a larger scale and help build coalitions that will take this even further. Cognitive crafting empowers you to view your work through a lens of purpose, instilling a sense of fulfilment and motivation in your professional journey.

While visiting NASA Space Centre in 1962, President John F. Kennedy was reported to have struck up a conversation with a janitor there. JFK asked the janitor what he was doing, and to his surprise, the janitor replied "Mr. President, I am helping put a man on the moon." Clearly, this janitor was able to perform an inspiring cognitive crafting exercise transcending the immediate nature of his job and linking his work to the overall organisational purpose and mission.

After completing an Impact Statement exercise, some may immediately work out the connections between their purpose and their work, area of study, or other life endeavours they are pursuing. This is very empowering and reassuring. Others may have difficulty in seeing the link between their roles and their purpose, or the link may not exist in the first place. Those may experience a sense of despair as they feel the need to continue in their jobs or fields of study for a variety of reasons while having to come to terms with the lack of purpose connectivity.

An accounts manager at an architectural firm, for example, may see their role as balancing the books and ensuring that accounts payable and receivable are done correctly and on time. The purpose of this accounts manager may be related to reducing the negative impact of human activities on climate change. At first glance, the connection between the role and purpose may not be that apparent, but a second look can reveal that this accounts manager may be able to mobilise their purpose by enabling their firm and the architects in it to perform their jobs in an environmentally friendly way. This includes advocacy for carbon-neutral materials and supply chains and even championing the environment through professional networks both within the organisation and outside it. Accountants are indeed important players when it comes to the environment.

Next Steps

In a nutshell, after completing your Impact Statement you can use life crafting to ensure that you live in harmony with your purpose. Beyond this, you can further enrich your purpose-driven life by engaging in volunteer work and participating in professional activities outside your organisation. If your current role starkly misaligns with your purpose, consider exploring alternative positions or capacities, whether within your current organisation or beyond. Ensuring positive career growth in the next step involves acquiring the necessary skills, capacities, and mindsets. This proactive approach allows you to navigate toward roles that resonate more closely with your purpose and contribute to your overall professional fulfilment.

7

Writing Impact Statements for Teams and Organisations

"There are only two ways to influence human behaviour; you can manipulate it or you can inspire it. Very few people or companies can clearly articulate why they do what they do. By why I mean your purpose, cause or belief — Why does your company exist?"

-Simon Sinek

As previously outlined, purpose and impact extend beyond individuals to encompass teams, businesses, and organisations. There is a growing recognition that having a well-defined sense of purpose is not only meaningful but also economically and commercially advantageous. Businesses and organisations articulating, embedding, and genuinely pursuing a clear and authentic higher purpose frequently experience enhanced customer loyalty and increased staff engagement. Purpose serves as a genuine driving force and a motivational factor for team members, not to mention its capacity to attract support and collaboration from partners and customers.

The Porter Novelli purpose tracker study[1] showed that a significant majority (93%) of employees surveyed assert that companies must, more than ever, prioritise purpose. This signifies a collective understanding among employees that business goes beyond mere profit-making. Notably, nearly nine-in-ten (88%) employees contend that it is no longer sufficient for companies to solely pursue financial gains; they must also contribute positively to society. As businesses pivot toward this evolved perspective on impact, employees recognise their role as essential stakeholders that businesses must consider. In fact, 95% of employees believe that businesses should benefit all stakeholders, not exclusively shareholders.

At a time when short-termism is rampant, purpose-driven organisations are in a much better position to make long-term decisions and investments and effectively articulate and justify those decisions to their stakeholders. This can be a clear advantage as many of the challenges, and indeed the opportunities, we encounter today demand long-term thinking to address and realise them.

That is why many leaders after articulating their Impact Statements start exploring the possibility of developing Impact Statements for their teams, businesses, and organisations. Just like the case of individuals, more and more leaders are realising the importance of articulating the purpose and impact of teams as well.

In this chapter, we will describe the process teams can use to develop their Impact Statements.

Team Impact Statement

For a group of people to effectively develop an Impact Statement for their team, business, or the organisation they lead, it is highly recommended that all the team members develop their individual Impact Statements first. This way they will all be familiar with the process and ready to take things to the next level. Working together on articulating an organisational or team purpose and impact is a great team-building exercise, which is an added benefit.

For the best experience and results, it is recommended that the team size working on the Impact Statement does not exceed 10 individuals. The team can be a functional group, such as a project team or sales department, or the leadership team of a bigger organisation such as a board of directors or a senior leadership team. As the team develop the organisational Impact Statement they are encouraged to engage with the wider community and seek feedback from others to ensure that what they will produce is both valid and accepted by the others.

The structure of a team's Impact Statement is similar to that of an individual Impact Statement replacing the "I am" Statement with We are Statement. We shall go through the process in some detail below.

"We Are" Statement

Just like the "I am" Statement, to write the "We are" Statement we will examine the Core Values and the life journey of the team or the organisation.

Team's Core Values

We will start by examining the team's Core Values.

Let's work:

1. Working independently, each team member is to identify the list of values that they believe resonate with the team or business and its culture from the list provided earlier in Chapter 3. The list is provided on the following pages for easy reference. This time, each value selected from the list needs to be written on a separate Post-it note or a small piece of paper.

Abundance
Acceptance
Accountability
Achievement
Adaptability
Adventure
Advocacy
Affection
Ambition
Appreciation
Authenticity
Autonomy
Awareness   **A**

Balance
Beauty
Belonging
Benevolence
Boldness
Brilliance   **B**

Calmness
Caring
Celebration
Challenge
Change
Charity
Cheerfulness
Clarity
Cleverness
Collaboration
Commitment
Communication
Community   **C**

Connection
Consistency
Contentment
Contribution
Curiosity
Cooperation
Courage
Creativity
Credibility
Curiosity   **C**

Decisiveness
Dedication
Dependability
Determination
Devotion
Discipline
Diversity   **D**

Empathy
Empowerment
Encouragement
Enthusiasm
Equality
Equity
Ethics
Excellence
Expressiveness   **E**

Fairness
Faith
Family
Flexibility
Focus   **F**

Forgiveness
Freedom
Friendship
Fun   **F**

Generosity
Grace
Gratitude
Growth   **G**

Happiness
Harmony
Health
Honesty
Hope
Humility
Humour   **H**

Impact
Inclusivity
Independence
Individuality
Innovation
Inspiration
Integrity
Intelligence
Intimacy
Intuition   **I**

Joy
Justice   **J**

Kindness
Knowledge   **K**

Leadership
Learning
Love
Loyalty **L**

Mindfulness
Motivation **M**

Nature
Neatness
Neutrality **N**

Open-mindedness
Optimism
Originality **O**

Patience
Passion
Peace
Perfection
Performance
Perseverance
Personal growth
Playfulness
Positivity
Power
Preparedness
Proactivity
Professionalism
Punctuality
Purpose **P**

Quality **Q**

Recognition
Reflection
Relationships
Reliability
Resilience
Resourcefulness
Respect
Responsibility
Responsiveness
Rigour
Risk-taking **R**

Safety
Security
Self-care
Self-discipline
Self-expression
Selflessness
Self-love
Service
Simplicity
Sincerity
Solitude
Spirituality
Stability
Status
Success
Support
Sustainability **S**

Teamwork
Thankfulness
Thoughtfulness
Timeliness **T**

Tolerance
Traditionalism
Trust
Truth **T**

Understanding
Unity
Uniqueness
Usefulness **U**

Versatility
Vision
Vitality **V**

Warmth
Wealth
Wellbeing
Winning
Wisdom
Wonder
Work ethic
Worthiness **W**

Youthfulness **Y**

Zeal
Zen **Z**

Note: Add any missing values below

2. Working together, the team members are to stick Post-it notes with the values they wrote on a board or the wall making sure that repeated values are noted and only 1 of them is kept. Then, the team is to work together to group all similar values in a way that makes sense to the team, collectively creating a maximum of five groupings, as done earlier in Chapter 3. Just like the case of individual values, if we have more than five groupings, the least important are to be dropped. The classification can be done in the space provided below.

3. Working together, the team members are to choose one word within each grouping that best represents the label for the entire group. These chosen labels represent the team's or the organisation's Core Values or are very close to being its Core Values.

1. _____

2. _____

3. _____

4. _____

5. _____

4. Working together, the team members bring the Core Values to life and activate them by adding a verb to each value to see what it looks like as an actionable Core Value.

1. _____

2. _____

3. _____

4. _____

5. _____

5. If your organisation has corporate core values, compare those to your selected team's Core Values and reflect on the similarities and differences.

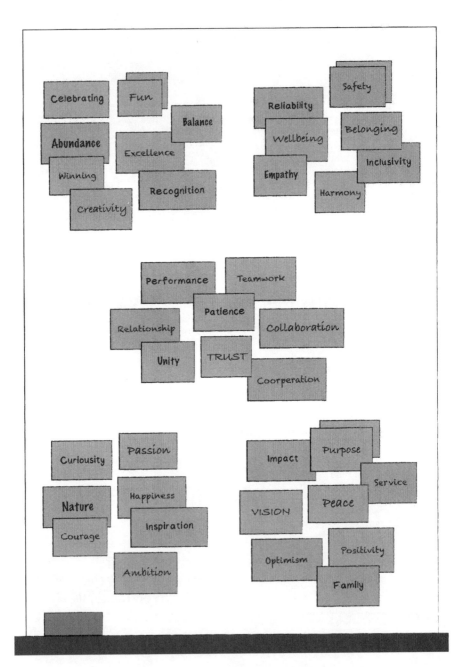

Team's Core Values Development Exercise

Your Team's Journey

In this section, you will explore your team's journey thus far with a focus on the Peak Moments in this journey. Your team may be part of a 200-year-old organisation, say the planning department of an ancient university, or a group of volunteers that was established 6 months ago to address the needs of a community. This exercise is valid in both cases. Ideally, but not necessarily, team members should have spent some time together within the team.

Let's work:

1. Individually, reflect on the 5 Peak Moments for your team or the organisation within which your team operates. Peak Moments are situations when you felt the team and/or the organisation were at their best, making you proud of the team and organisation and the impact they are having on the world. These could be moments you were directly involved in or not. They may even have happened well before you joined the team or the organisation.

2. For each Peak Moment you identify, on a Post-it note write:

   When did the Peak Moment take place?
   What was the event or the situation?
   Why did it stand out for you?
   What impact did that have on others?
   What values were your team or organisation honouring?
   How did the event make you feel?

3. Now, draw a straight timeline on a board or a wall and ask the participating team members to stick their Peak Moments chronologically along the line.

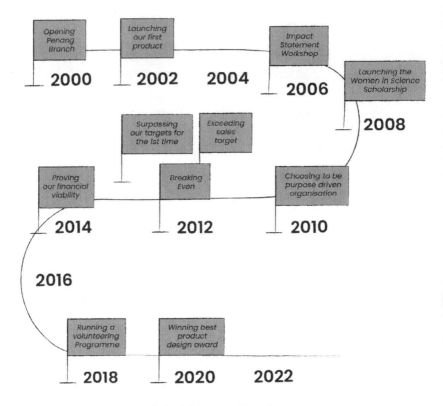

Team's Peak Moments Time Line

4. The participants can now read all the Peak Moments identified by the team members and arranged along the timeline and reflect on them. Observe if any Peak Moments are selected by more than one team member, these shared moments provide additional insight into what makes the team or the organisation what it is. Participants can have conversations around these Peak Moments. Check if these shared moments are remembered differently or from different angles.

Now, reflecting together on the team's Core Values and Peak Moments, decide the team's "We are" Statement. Below are some examples:

We are Statement	The Team/ Organisation
We are life changers.	A Foundation that trains differently able youths and gets them ready for jobs.
We are authenticity enablers.	A Public Relations agency.
We are storytellers.	Marketing department.
We are risk mitigators.	Audit department.
We are fiscal wizards.	Finance department.
We are wealth creators.	An Investment company.
We are future shapers.	A University.

Write your team's "We are" Statement below:

We are

Let's reflect:

1. Share your Core Values and "We are" Statement with 5 stakeholders, customers, clients, partners, or other colleagues and seek their feedback. Ask them:

   ► *What are their thoughts?*

   ► *Do your team's Core Values and We are Statement describe the team's ethos and what it does or delivers well?*

► *Do they have any alternative suggestions for your Core Values? Outline the essence of these conversations below.*

2. How do you feel about this exercise?

3. Are there any discoveries and/or surprises?

Team and Organisation Purpose

Just like individual purpose, teams of people can find the purpose of their teams or even their business and organisation using the ikigai concept. The group working on articulating the purpose will need to create 4 lists outlining.

1.   What the world needs that your team or organisation is passionate and determined to deliver.

2.   The strengths, skills, capabilities, resources, and networks that your team or organisation has access to.

3.   The functions and objectives that your team or organisation are set up to achieve.

4.   What people at your team or organisation love doing.

The team will need to find common areas between these 4 lists as this will be an indication of their team's or organisation's purpose.

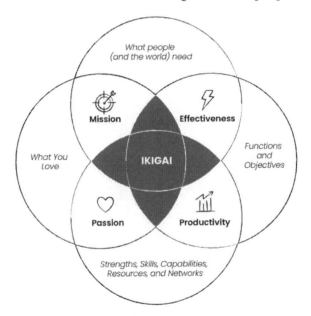

Ikigai for Teams and Organisations

Below are worked examples for the 4 lists developed for a university.

The World Needs

1. Peace & Happiness
2. Understanding
3. Purpose-driven leadership
4. Meaning
5. Environmental solutions
6. Justice & Equality
7. Inclusive technology
8. Economic opportunities
9. Hope
10. Sustainable development

Functions & Objectives

1. Educating people
2. Performing research
3. Creating knowledge
4. Advocating policy
5. Community engagement
6. Global engagement
7. Social responsibility
8. Promoting culture
9. Fostering innovation
10. Building purpose-driven leaders

IKIGAI

We Love

1. Adding value
2. Empowering people through finding purpose
3. Making a difference
4. Discovering solutions
5. Sharing knowledge
6. Challenging paradigms
7. Transforming life
8. Providing opportunities
9. Supporting women
10. Building partnerships

Our Strengths, Skills, Resources, Networks

1. Purpose-driven
2. Research excellence
3. Community influence
4. Successful alumni
5. Employers networks
6. Expert faculties
7. Motivated students
8. Research excellence
9. Effective teaching
10. Global presence

Reflecting on the lists above, the team working on articulating the purpose of this university observed that two themes were repeating, in different manifestations, through these 4 lists, namely:

1. *Purpose, meaning, and purpose-driven leadership.*

2. *The need for the promotion of equality and sustainability through education, research, advocacy, and partnership.*

Examining these two themes closely, the team felt a sense of agreement with this finding. They progressed towards crafting the Purpose Statement below:

Our purpose is to cultivate purpose-driven leaders dedicated to fostering a sustainable, equitable, and enjoyable world.

Let's work:

Now, together with your team members, do the same exercise for your team, department, or organisation. Complete the four lists below:

The World Needs

1. _____
2. _____
3. _____
4. _____
5. _____
6. _____
7. _____
8. _____
9. _____
10. _____

Functions & Objectives

1. _____
2. _____
3. _____
4. _____
5. _____
6. _____
7. _____
8. _____
9. _____
10. _____

IKIGAI

We Love

1. _____
2. _____
3. _____
4. _____
5. _____
6. _____
7. _____
8. _____
9. _____
10. _____

Our Strengths, Skills, Resources, Networks

1. _____
2. _____
3. _____
4. _____
5. _____
6. _____
7. _____
8. _____
9. _____
10. _____

To inspire you, below are some Purpose Statement:

Purpose Statement	The Team/ Organisation
Our purpose is to spark courageous exploration to inspire a better world.	A School
Our purpose is to organise the world's information and make it universally accessible and useful.	Google
Our purpose is to transform data and trends into stories and help leaders make data-informed decisions.	Planning Department
Our purpose is to cultivate purpose-driven leaders dedicated to fostering a sustainable, equitable, and enjoyable world.	A University

Purpose Statement of the Alice Smith School in Kuala Lumpur
(included with permission from Alice Smith School)

Write your Purpose below:

Our purpose is

_____

_____

_____

_____

Let's reflect: ☑

1. Share the Purpose Statement of your team or organisation with at least 5 customers, clients, stakeholders, and/or other staff members and seek their feedback. What are their thoughts? Does the statement match how your team, business, and organisation are perceived? Do they have any alternative suggestions?

2. How does the team feel about the exercise of articulating their team, business, or organisational purpose?

3. How does your team's "We are" Statement connect with the team's Purpose Statement? Is there a natural flow between the two?

4. Are there any discoveries and/or surprises?

_____
_____
_____
_____
_____
_____
_____
_____
_____
_____
_____
_____
_____
_____
_____
_____
_____
_____
_____

Now, put the "We are" Statement and the Purpose Statement together and write your team/organisation Impact Statement:

We are _____

Our purpose is _____

_____

_____

Mobilising Your Purpose into Positive Impact

After crafting the "We are" Statement and Purpose Statement, it would be truly rewarding if the team developed a stronger commitment to aligning their business objectives to the mobilisation of the purpose of the organisation. It is important to emphasise here that purpose is simultaneously about individual and organisational fulfilment on one hand, and service to others on the other. Therefore aligning business objectives with the mobilising of purpose should be viewed as a strategy that makes business sense, rather than a costly afterthought.

Many businesses now recognise that authentically aligning their objectives and operations with environmentally sustainable practices, for example, is paying dividends in employee engagement, customer loyalty, policymaker support, and cost reduction. This can have the direct impact of potentially creating an atmosphere in which the cost of doing business is lowered. Learning from this, and as purpose becomes the ultimate arbiter of all essential business decisions, purpose-driven organisations can benefit from developing more trust in their brands lowering the transactional cost for them and capitalising on the associated goodwill.

While this section is not intended to present a comprehensive business strategy and goalsetting methodology, it is meant to reassure and inspire leaders who are keen on creating purpose-driven teams, organisations, and businesses and provide the philosophy, language, and thought process for adopting purpose-driven planning and decision-making mechanisms.

Purpose-Driven Leadership

I would like to introduce here the concept of purpose-driven leadership where the role of leaders is seen as building, enhancing, growing and preserving 5 primary types of capital: human, social, emotional, natural, and economic. This represents a more holistic and sustainable approach to the practice of leadership focusing on delivering the business objectives while mobilising its purpose into a positive impact on others. This concept is depicted graphically in the figure shown below. Leaders can harness the deep sense of purpose they cultivate in their organisations as a driving force to leverage these 5 capitals at their disposal to achieve success for their teams, businesses, and organisations while making the world a better place for everyone. The balanced combination of success and impact will result in sustainable flourishing for those involved and associated with the business.

Purpose-driven leaders deploy these 5 capitals in an integrated fashion so that they complement, enhance, and leverage each other for more effective and impactful results. As organisations perform their strategic planning, resource allocation, and goal-setting functions, and as team members set their key performance indicators (KPIs) it will be empowering to consider the utilisation and creation of these capitals as the background to all these processes. A short description of these 5 capitals is given herewith:

1. **Human capital** refers to the knowledge, skills and capabilities that a team or an organisation has access to or would like to develop, promote, and deliver. Purpose-driven leadership prioritises the development of human capital in a manner that creates more success, impact, and flourishing. This implies strategic investment in people to develop and upskill them to deliver the business and organisational objectives while pursuing the higher purpose for the organisation and the people associated with it.

2. **Social capital** is the positive relationships and networks that a team or an organisation have access to or would like to nurture and develop in order to simultaneously deliver on both the higher purpose and the business objectives. Social capital can be highly potent as it serves as a multiplier of all other types of capital.

3. **Emotional capital** is the ability to assess and positively influence emotions to motivate and inspire others in order to align business objectives with a worthy higher purpose and create an emotional commitment to delivering that. It also refer to the emotional connection that customers may have with a brand, service, or a product. Often the availability of emotional capital can be the bottleneck to delivering on the organisational strategy. When

people are inspired, motivated, and believe in the worthiness of the organisational purpose, they can move mountains.

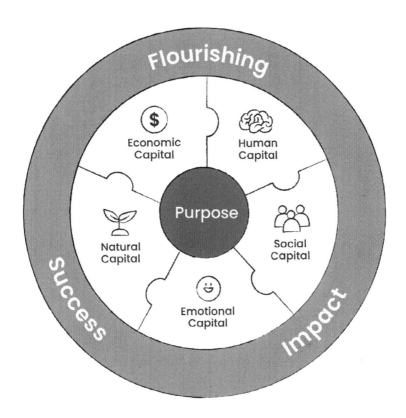

Purpose-Driven Leadership Model

4. **Natural capital** refers to our environment and natural resources we all share and how the presence and operation of a team and organisation help not only preserve but also enhance and improve this capital that we hold in trust for our future generations. It is essential that organisational strategies and goals outline how they will actively enhance and improve the environment in which they operate and we all live. As mentioned earlier, holding the higher moral ground in this realm is the right thing to do on multiple levels including making clear business sense, by potentially reducing the cost of operation in the long term, as well as building goodwill and brand trust.

5. **Economic capital** is the financial resources that a team or organisation has access to and how they can be used to create more value and help further the mobilisation of purpose into positive impact. Economic capital represents the bloodline of an organisation and directly affects its ability to honour its obligations, realise its objectives, and deliver on its purpose. Being skilled in the management of this capital is a prerequisite for the successful leadership of organisations large and small.

Viewing the business decision-making and goal-setting processes through the lens of the above 5 capitals and leveraging them to mobilise the organisational and individual purpose can be an effective way to develop plans and strategies that not only deploy resources but also inspire people to go on the journey of becoming a purpose-driven team, business, and organisation.

Epilogue

Where Do We Go from Here?

"There is only one thing stronger than all the armies of the world: and that is an idea whose time has come."

-Victor Hugo

As argued in this book, compelling evidence suggests that humanity is currently standing at the precipice of a pivotal moment in its history. The culmination of our technological advancements demands a parallel development of our human potential—to discover our purpose, nurture our wisdom, and enhance our capacity for wisdom, love, care, and kindness. Unleashing this human potential represents the existential challenge of our age; it is the sole path available for us to remain relevant and able to effectively employ our technology to tackle our grand challenges, rather than succumb to some of the dystopian fears that loom. While advanced technologies, particularly Artificial Intelligence (AI), are presenting us with unprecedented challenges and opportunities, they are making it clear that the ultimate value that humans add to life is through their sense of purpose and emotional labour. This is why I am firmly convinced that the significance of investing in cultivating a profound sense of purpose is an idea whose time has arrived.

Whether you have always reflected on your purpose, or you are exploring this important topic with a fresh pair of eyes, thank you choosing to have this book as part of your purpose journey. Discovering our purpose and mobilising it into a positive impact on the world is a lifelong continuous endeavour that will require ongoing tending. I really hope that you will remain committed to this worthwhile practice.

As individuals, parents, leaders, and partners in the human project, cultivating our own sense of purpose and helping those under our care cultivate theirs, as well as building our businesses and organisations to be purpose-driven will be a defining factor in our success, happiness, impact, and flourishing.

I hope this book will be a helpful resource for you as you discover your purpose and help others discover theirs. As you do that, I would love to hear from you and learn how are you getting on and how are you mobilising your purpose into a positive impact as I know for a fact that the world needs you, your superpowers, and your magic. You can reach me at **mushtak.alatabi@gmail.com**

Dream Big. Be Different. Have Fun.

Appendix I
Impact Statement Playbook

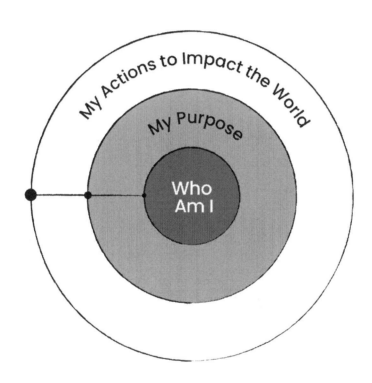

Self-Awareness, Purpose, and Impact

Impact Statement Structure

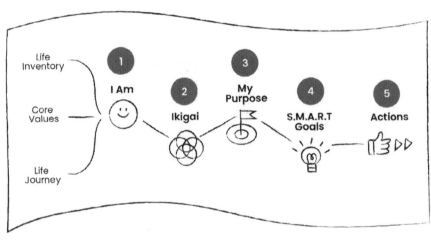

Roadmap for Writing Your Impact Statement

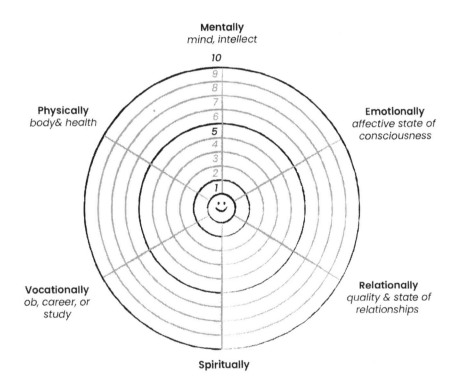

Mentally
mind, intellect

Physically
body& health

Emotionally
*affective state of
consciousness*

Vocationally
*ob, career, or
study*

Relationally
*quality & state of
relationships*

Spiritually

Your Wheel of Life

Abundance	Connection	Forgiveness
Acceptance	Consistency	Freedom
Accountability	Contentment	Friendship
Achievement	Contribution	Fun **F**
Adaptability	Curiosity	
Adventure	Cooperation	Generosity
Advocacy	Courage	Grace
Affection	Creativity	Gratitude
Ambition	Credibility	Growth **G**
Appreciation	Curiosity **C**	
Authenticity		Happiness
Autonomy	Decisiveness	Harmony
Awareness **A**	Dedication	Health
	Dependability	Honesty
Balance	Determination	Hope
Beauty	Devotion	Humility
Belonging	Discipline	Humour **H**
Benevolence	Diversity **D**	
Boldness		Impact
Brilliance **B**	Empathy	Inclusivity
	Empowerment	Independence
Calmness	Encouragement	Individuality
Caring	Enthusiasm	Innovation
Celebration	Equality	Inspiration
Challenge	Equity	Integrity
Change	Ethics	Intelligence
Charity	Excellence	Intimacy
Cheerfulness	Expressiveness **E**	Intuition **I**
Clarity		
Cleverness	Fairness	Joy **J**
Collaboration	Faith	Justice
Commitment	Family	
Communication	Flexibility	Kindness **K**
Community **C**	Focus **F**	Knowledge

List of Core Values

Leadership
Learning
Love
Loyalty   **L**

Mindfulness   **M**
Motivation

Nature
Neatness
Neutrality   **N**

Open-mindedness
Optimism
Originality   **O**

Patience
Passion
Peace
Perfection
Performance
Perseverance
Personal growth
Playfulness
Positivity
Power
Preparedness
Proactivity
Professionalism
Punctuality
Purpose   **P**

Quality   **Q**

Recognition
Reflection
Relationships
Reliability
Resilience
Resourcefulness
Respect
Responsibility
Responsiveness
Rigour
Risk-taking   **R**

Safety
Security
Self-care
Self-discipline
Self-expression
Selflessness
Self-love
Service
Simplicity
Sincerity
Solitude
Spirituality
Stability
Status
Success
Support
Sustainability   **S**

Teamwork
Thankfulness
Thoughtfulness
Timeliness   **T**

Tolerance
Traditionalism
Trust
Truth   **T**

Understanding
Unity
Uniqueness
Usefulness   **U**

Versatility
Vision
Vitality   **V**

Warmth
Wealth
Wellbeing
Winning
Wisdom
Wonder
Work ethic
Worthiness   **W**

Youthfulness   **Y**

Zeal
Zen   **Z**

Note: Add any missing values below

List of Core Values

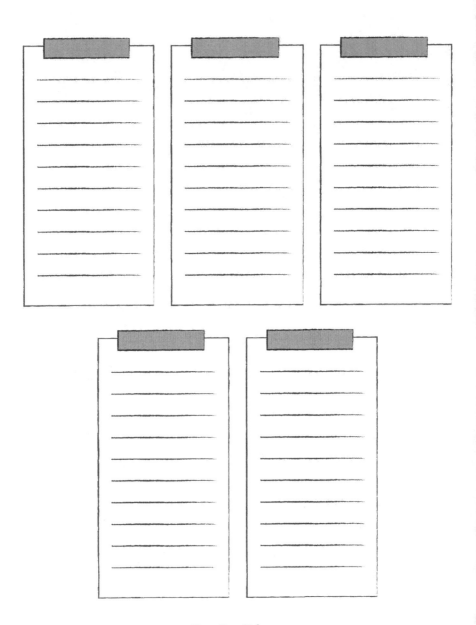

Your Core Values

Top 5 Core Values.

1. _____

2. _____

3. _____

4. _____

5. _____

Activation of Core Values.

1. _____

2. _____

3. _____

4. _____

5. _____

Birth (Age)

Your Life-Line & Peak Moments

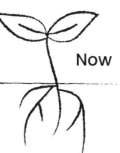

Now

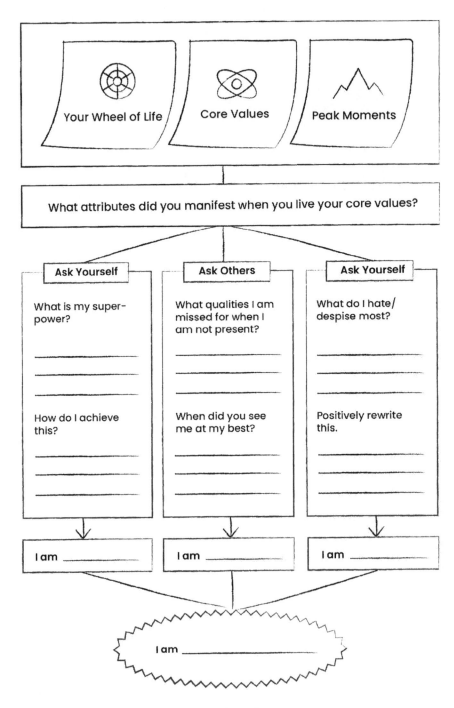

Finding Your "I Am" Statement

I am

Your "I Am" Statement

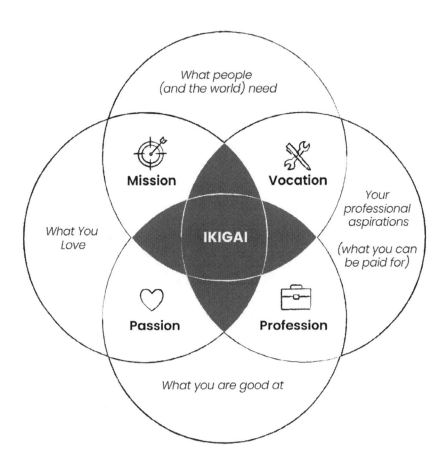

Discovering Your Purpose (Ikigai)

The World Needs

1. _____
2. _____
3. _____
4. _____
5. _____
6. _____
7. _____
8. _____
9. _____
10. _____

I'd Like to be Paid For

1. _____
2. _____
3. _____
4. _____
5. _____
6. _____
7. _____
8. _____
9. _____
10. _____

IKIGAI

I Love

1. _____
2. _____
3. _____
4. _____
5. _____
6. _____
7. _____
8. _____
9. _____
10. _____

I'm Good At

1. _____
2. _____
3. _____
4. _____
5. _____
6. _____
7. _____
8. _____
9. _____
10. _____

Your Purpose (Ikigai)

I am
_____

My purpose is
_____

_____

_____

Your Purpose Statement

	Specific	Measurable	Attainable	Relevant	Time-Bound
Description	What do you want to accomplish? Who needs to be included?	How to measure progress & know that you have achieved your goal?	What skills, resources, and networks do you need to achieve your goal?	How relevant is this to your purpose?	When will this goal be achieved?
Example	Improve mathematics for children by running technology based workshops.	Traning 1000 children aged 10-15 years so that they can pass mathematics standard test.	1. Organisational skills. 2. Collaboration with NGOs. 3. Attracting volunteers.	My purpose is to enable children to achieve their full potential through mastering mathematics.	12 months from the start date of the project.
	Now it's your turn! Fill in the blank with your goals				
12 Months Goal					
36 Months Goal					

Your S.M.A.R.T Goals

I am

My purpose is

I (will/ dedicate my life for/ endeavour to)

Your Impact Statement

Appendix II
Life Crafting

	Task	Percentage of Time %	Strengths Alignment	Level of Enjoyment
1				
2				
3				
4				
5				
6				
7				
8				
9				
10				

The Top 10 Tasks You Spend Most of Your Time Performing

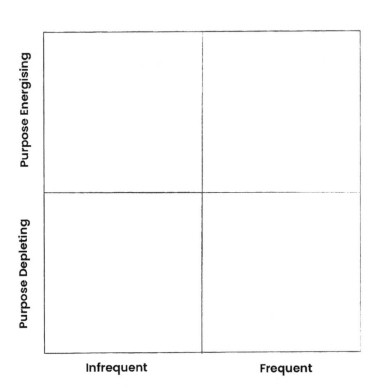

The Visual Social/ Professional Universe

Reflections and Notes

Reflections and Notes

Reflections and Notes

Reflections and Notes

Reflections and Notes

Reflections and Notes

Reflections and Notes

Reflections and Notes

Reflections and Notes

Reflections and Notes

Notes

Chapter 1: Why Purpose?

1. Frankl, V. E., 2006. Man's Search for Meaning. Boston: Beacon Press.

2. Damon, W., 2008. The Path to Purpose: How Young People Find Their Calling in Life. New York: Free Press.

3. Quinn, R. E. and Thakor, A. V., 2019. The Economics of Higher Purpose. Oakland: Berrett-Koehler Publishers, Inc.

4. Dhingra, N., Emmett, J., Samo, A., and Schaninger, B., 2020. Igniting Individual Purpose in Times of Crisis. McKinsey Quarterly.

5. McKinsey Global Institute. 2017. Jobs Lost, Jobs Gained: Workforce Transformations in A Time of Automation.

6. Varoufakis, Y., 2023. Technofeudalism: What Killed Capitalism. Jonathan Cape and BH.

7. Bostrom, N., 2014. Superintelligence: Paths, Dangers, Strategies. London: Oxford University Press.

Chapter 4: Discovering Your Purpose

1. Damon, W., 2008. The Path to Purpose: How Young People Find Their Calling in Life. New York: Free Press.

2. Hall, D., Rangunathan, T., Tan, Y.S., Wong, W.L., Dass, S.C., Low, J., Lee, C.P., Namasivayam, S.N., Choong, S., and Al-Atabi, M. 2023. Impact of Defining ikigai in Developing Future-Ready University Graduates with Self-Leadership Skills: A Whole University Mixed-

Methods Study During COVID-19. Asia Pacific Journal of Education. Volume 43, Pages 660-691.

Chapter 6: Crafting A Purpose-Driven Life

1. Wrzesniewski, A., Berg, J. M., and Dutton, J. E., 2010. Managing Yourself: Turn the Job You Have into the Job You Want. Harvard Business Review.

2. Waldinger, R., and Schulz, M., 2023. The Good Life and How to Live it: Lessons from the World's Longest Study on Happiness. London: Penguin Random House.

Chapter 7: Writing Impact Statements for Teams and Organisations

1. PN Purpose Tracker. 2020. Employee Perspectives on Responsible Leadership During Crisis.

Made in the USA
Columbia, SC
13 March 2024